MENTORING MARRIAGES

*Use your experience
of the ups and downs
of married life
to support other couples*

Harry Benson

MONARCH
BOOKS

Oxford, UK, and Grand Rapids, Michigan, USA

First published in the UK in 2005 by Monarch Books
(a publishing imprint of Lion Hudson plc),
Mayfield House, 256 Banbury Road, Oxford, OX2 7DH
Tel: +44 (0) 1865 302750   Fax: +44 (0) 1865 302757
Email: monarch@lionhudson.com
www.lionhudson.com

UK ISBN 1 85424 699 2
US ISBN 0 8254 6087 5

Distributed by:
UK: Marston Book Services Ltd, PO Box 269,
Abingdon, Oxon OX14 4YN;
USA: Kregel Publications, PO Box 2607,
Grand Rapids, Michigan 49501.
Worldwide co-edition produced by Lion Hudson plc,
Mayfield House, 256 Banbury Road, Oxford OX2 7DH
Tel: +44 (0) 1865 302750   Fax: +44 (0) 1865 302757
Email: monarch@lionhudson.com

British Library Cataloguing Data
A catalogue record for this book is available
from the British Library.

Book design and production for the publishers by Lion Hudson plc.
Printed in Great Britain.

Contents

Commendations

"*Harry Benson makes a unique contribution, as he couples a sharp academic mind with a practical passion to see married couples build the best possible foundations for marriage. He explains the 'why' and 'how to' of marriage mentoring. Benson doesn't say marriage is a bed of roses. He says mentoring will make a dramatic difference, and I agree with him. This book will be a divorce-buster!*"
Jonathan Booth, Director, Care for the Family UK

"*The most important new idea to revitalise marriage is couple mentoring. One couple in a healthy marriage is trained to assist another to prepare, enrich or restore a marriage. This strategy is fun and deeply rewarding, and can almost eliminate divorce! Harry Benson learned from American churches the power of mentoring and has successfully transplanted it onto British soil. More importantly, he has written a superb book, 'Mentoring marriages', which is a must-read for anyone interested in revitalising marriage – on either side of the Atlantic.*"
Mike McManus, President, Marriage Savers USA

Acknowledgements

So many people have helped Kate and me to transform our marriage from a place of despair and ignorance to a life of vibrant colour. Thank you, all.

- Steve and Ali Bryan were there for us at the moment of reckoning and got us started on the road to recovery. David and Ruth Thorne sent us off for a life-changing marriage weekend. Nicky and Sila Lee inspired us with ideas and their path as marriage educators. Arthur and Jenny Dickson have lurked in the background as our informal mentors, on whose shoulders we occasionally lean. Ian and Claire Nelson encourage us so much as friends.

In my work as a marriage and relationship educator, I have been deeply influenced by a handful of men and women of great vision, enthusiasm, warmth and humility. I keep learning more and more from you.

- Mike McManus has flown the flag for mentoring in the US and inspired me to do likewise in the UK. Countless thousands of American families are the richer for his and Harriet's single-minded determination to turn back the tide of family breakdown. Like Mike, Chris Grimshaw is another modern-day Wilberforce, who has almost single-handedly put relationship education on the public agenda in the UK. It's fantastic to have somebody of such drive alongside. Dave and Liz Percival provide wisdom and encouragement when they are not running www.2-in-2-1.co.uk, the most informative marriage web site in the UK.

- In getting going with mentoring, I am especially grateful to Andrew and Ros Wallis, who generously took the risk of letting Kate and me run riot with our new programmes at Bristol Vineyard church. Thanks to my lovely trustees at Bristol Community Family Trust for keeping me on the straight and narrow – Richard, Anne, Ann and Siobhan. And a giant hug to Claire Cox, who takes all the administrative niceties off my desk, is always smiling, and has never complained that the charity never seems to have more than three months' cash left. Thanks as well to the many Bristol couples who often doubted how much they had to offer as mentors, yet dared to have a go.

On the technical side, few of the ideas in this book are original. I stand on the shoulders of giants. I hope I've done them justice with the way I've presented and reorganised these ideas.

- I am especially influenced, as you will realise, by the work of Scott Stanley and Howard Markman. Several of the practical skills and principles in this book are my adaptation from their PREP programme, currently the best-researched programme anywhere in the world. I learned so much from Diane Sollee's wonderful Smartmarriages conference – I recommend you go. Mike

McManus and Barbara Markey got me going on mentoring and I've taken it from there.

- I am enormously grateful to Tony Collins at Monarch for seeing the need to publish a book on mentoring marriages in the first place. His many constructive comments have helped me remove some of the sharp edges from my early drafts and hopefully made the book more readable.

Bless you, Jonathan Booth and Dave and Liz Percival, who commented generously on my first draft and encouraged me to change the order of the book. Bless you, Kate, for commenting generously on my second draft and encouraging me to rewrite the entire book! I did.

Finally, and most importantly, thank you to those closest to me. Mum, you always did what you thought was best for me; and you taught me about loyalty. My late grandparents, Jack and Ruth, you were there for me throughout my childhood; and you taught me about commitment. Kate, you stuck with me when I had no idea how to be your friend. And you stick with me now when I occasionally forget. Our marriage is unrecognisable and unthinkable compared to ten years ago. I love spending today with you and I look forward to very many tomorrows. Benson kids, you're fantastically wonderful – Rosie, Polly, Gracie, Sizzle, Charlie and Johnnie. And I am more grateful than I can say to Jesus. You give me everything I need. I was lost and now I'm found.

Harry Benson
Bristol UK

Chapter 1   # Rebuilding family life

Rebuilding family life

We have experienced astonishing changes in the developed world since the end of the Second World War. During the last 60 years, we have become far more worldly-wise and well travelled. We've become a far more affluent society. We have far greater access to an amazing array of foods and consumer products. All in all, we have far greater freedom and choices than our parents ever had.

But that same sense of greater individual freedom has also affected the way we live as families. Sixty years ago, extended family and local community social patterns largely determined the way individuals lived their lives. Lifelong marriage was an expected norm. Almost all children had married parents. Family breakdown was relatively rare.

Today, personal rights and needs largely determine the way individuals live their lives. Lifelong marriage is just one of a range of options. In the UK, for example, nearly half of all children are now born to unmarried parents. Family breakdown is rampant. The consequence is that one in four young adults now come from broken homes.

Sixty years on, our world may look spectacularly better for consumers. But it looks spectacularly worse for families.

I am a child of divorce. My parents divorced back in the

early 1960s, when I was just three years old and when divorce was still rare in Britain. My mum brought up my brother and me largely on her own, heroically even, until she remarried some years later. I spent much of my childhood from age seven onwards at boarding school.

These early experiences affected me profoundly. I don't blame my parents for their choices because I wasn't in their shoes. However, I did feel a sense of abandonment by the people I should have been able to trust most. As I grew up, I dealt with this by taking the safe route of not relying on anybody. Sooner or later, everybody lets you down. I shut down emotionally and became very independent. Being so closed off meant that relationships were hard to come by, with the result that I had few friends at school. *"It's better not to feel"* was one part of my plan. *"I can succeed on my own"* was another part.

The excellent education I received allowed my plan to work brilliantly until I was 34. By then I had built two successful careers – entirely on my own, of course – first as a Navy helicopter pilot and then as a businessman in Asia. Along the way, I had managed to get married to a lovely girl called Kate. We had two little girls.

At that point, in 1994, to the outside world we probably looked like a happy and successful young family. To us on the inside, we were anything but. My inability to feel or relate had finally caught up with me.

For eight years of married life, Kate had put up with a committed but unresponsive husband. I remember feeling so confused each time she told me she wanted more from our marriage. I was convinced I was providing so much, yet I simply had no idea how to be a friend or husband. I remember wondering from time to time how I could ever tell whether our marriage was any good or not. I soon found out: Kate told me she had finally had enough. Like so many couples, we had grown further and further apart. We were living like flat-mates. Either I started talking to my wife and being her friend, or our marriage was history.

At the time of writing, Kate and I have now been married for 18 years and we have six children. We have rebuilt a marriage that is unrecognisably better than ever before. We still have some pretty awful moments when married life can seem bleak: old habits die hard. But what we have now that we didn't have before is the great majority of the time spent enjoying each other's company in confidence that we have what it takes for a lifetime together. It's not been down to chance. It's taken time, effort and commitment.

Kate and I were fortunate in that both of us wanted to make our marriage work. We are both committed to a life together. That has given us the time and motivation to learn and relearn the skills and attitudes needed to make a marriage work well. Much of this has come through the generosity, love and role-modelling shown us by other married couples.

Before Kate and I started confronting our marriage difficulties, we would never have sat down as a couple and talked about our marriage. It simply didn't occur to us. Nobody *talks* about their marriage; it's private. Off-limits. No wonder everybody is so surprised when close friends announce they are getting a divorce.

But we *should* talk to our friends about our marriage. More today than ever before. So much of our opinion on what marriage should be like comes from what we saw when we were growing up. More than ever, that comes from the only example we have ever seen at close quarters, our parents. The rest is digested from snippets in magazines, books, TV and films. Those views are always second-hand. Unless we have extended families to watch at close quarters, we are entirely reliant on a solitary role model, our parents' marriage, for the only direct exposure we have to married life – for better, for worse.

Talking to married friends allows us to multiply our direct exposure to how marriage works. Many of us have only seen it fail – whether through divorce or conflict. Knowing what fails is not the same as knowing what works. Hence second marriages are twice as likely to fail as first marriages. Failure doesn't tell us how to succeed.

We need to discover again the secrets of marriage and family life. What's normal? What's healthy? Should we have such big ups and downs? Is it OK to leave an issue buried and unresolved? How do others deal with difficult issues? Are others like us, or are we uniquely odd? How come we've never asked anyone these questions?

I am certain that Kate and I wouldn't have gone through anything like the marital hell we went through if we had learned some skills and been supported when we started our life together. We would have been so much more aware of our differences and potential problems and so much better equipped to handle them constructively.

I am equally certain that it was when we learned some skills and had informal support from older married couples that our marriage started to turn around. We could not have blundered by accident into the new level of intimacy and romance that renders our marriage today unrecognisable from what it was before. Chance and randomness lead to chaos and disorder. We needed to find processes that work.

Of course it's also important to remember that most marriages still do last a lifetime. If we teach nobody and support nobody, the world won't stop going round. Most couples do fine. Yet most break-ups are almost certainly avoidable. Most couples could have far stronger and more satisfying relationships than they think. If only they knew how.

Well, that certainly applies to us. And there are all too many Harrys and Kates who shouldn't have to go through what we've gone through. Every one of them can have so much more.

Being extended family

Having gone through the horror of near-divorce, I left business to become a full-time marriage educator. One of the most important things I've learned since then is the positive influence of extended family. Extended family networks – grandparents, uncles and aunts, cousins – offer three major qualities:

- They offer a source of values, many of which we take on automatically: *"This is what's important to us in our family."*
- They offer ongoing opportunities to learn at first hand from other family members: *"This is the way we do things in our family."*
- They offer ongoing opportunities for encouragement, support and ideas from other family members: *"This is who we can talk to and what we talk about in our family."*

The demise of the extended family is not just a modern myth. Nor am I pining for a glorious past under the mysterious illusion that somehow we had it better then. There is very good research evidence that extended family support has been eroded dramatically since the 1970s. For example, one major UK study now shows that a huge number of those who get old or ill, who would previously have been looked after at home, are now being looked after by the state. I'll talk more about this later. It's also surely not a coincidence that Spain and Italy, where extended family is still the norm, have by far the lowest divorce rates in Europe.

What I think we've lost as a society by moving away from extended family is our best source of values, learning and support. When it comes to how we "do" family ourselves, we no longer have an anchor to which to attach ourselves. We take our lead from TV soaps, from Hollywood films, from celebrities.

The result is that we no longer value marriage especially. It's now just one of many "lifestyle choices". We no longer have marriages to scrutinise and from which to learn what works. Without extended family, we no longer have other couples to support us and reassure us about our marriage or relationships. We can only ever talk about marriage with our friends when things are going wrong.

So we have thrown off the yoke of extended family and become "free". On the outside, we are economically richer in material choices, material opportunities and material comforts. Yet we have failed to find a new source of values, learning and support to replace that of extended family. On the inside, we are emotionally and relationally poorer in our well-being, in our relationships, in our communities. The evidence is all around us – huge increases in broken homes, mental health problems, educational problems, social dysfunction and crime.

Support couples – also called mentor couples – are an attempt to replace what has been lost. We cannot go back to a cosy world of supportive extended family. Maybe in a generation, our own children will choose differently. But, for now, we need to regain and re-establish what was lost. Being a support couple is a way to do this. Simply through spending time with a couple and sharing their experience, support couples demonstrate the value of a marriage, provide a source of learning and offer a source of support.

Marriage and relationship support is not rocket science. Uncles and aunts don't have to be counsellors or professionals to be effective.

- It doesn't take an expert to spend time with a couple and show them that their marriage is valued
- It doesn't take an expert to talk about our own longer experience of marriage, with its ups and downs
- It doesn't take an expert to get a couple to talk about their own shorter experience, with its ups and downs.

Professionals can sometimes act like a modern version of witch doctors, surrounding their work with lofty language and complex theories. It is a nonsense that you have to be specially trained or specially skilled to make a difference to marriages. It is a nonsense that you have to be tightly supervised like counsellors.

Just as any married couple can be an uncle and aunt, a little education makes you a well-informed uncle and aunt. In much the same way, more or less any married couple can be a support couple. You don't need to have a fantastic marriage. In fact, it helps if you're less than perfect and have survived the stress of the bad times as well as enjoyed the good. You need only have a "good enough" marriage and care that other people do too. A little education then makes you a well-informed support couple.

The triumph of experience over hope

The writer Samuel Johnson famously quipped that second marriages were "the triumph of hope over experience". The hope is that a second marriage will work in spite of the experience of a failed first marriage. This time it's different. We're in love. Disaster won't happen to us. Yet two in three second marriages still fail.

Much the same could be said today about couples getting married for the first time. Couples set out with great hope for their future in spite of the experience of failed marriages, negative statistics and cynical expectations all around them. They say they're different. They're in love. Disaster won't happen to them. Yet one in three first marriages still fail.

Being a support couple is all about sharing the experience of a successful marriage – with its downs as well as its ups – with couples starting out with such hope. Hope is a great place to start a life together. But hope is no longer enough on its own. Experience is what turns hope into triumph.

How to use this book

I've written this book primarily to show any ordinary married couple how to provide really effective support to a couple starting their life together. Using the same principles, you can also be a support couple to stepfamilies, those coming out of prison, or couples in crisis. In every case, the principles are the same. Those who have been there spend time with those who are there now.

If you choose to overlook a few specific issues that apply only to those getting married, the principles in the book should also prove helpful for any couples at any other stage of life.

Part One is really the meat of the book. It's a short course in how to be a good enough support/mentor couple. Some of my colleagues in the UK have found people more willing to become a *"support couple"* than a *"mentor couple"*. To me, the meaning is the same. But if a different word encourages more couples to have a go, then I'm for it. So although I will occasionally refer to the process as *"mentoring"* – *"supporting"* doesn't quite work – I shall be using the term *"support couple"* from here on.

Chapter 2 gives you an introduction to what you need to know. I tell you why support couples are ordinary couples. You don't need a perfect marriage or great expertise. I hope it'll give you enough confidence to get started. You'll see how straightforward the process is and why you really don't need any special skills. When you need more detail, just dip into the relevant chapter.

Learning how to recognise good and bad patterns of behaviour is where you can start to add extra value. Chapter 3 looks at the bad habits or patterns that are the most important determinants of whether a marriage will last or not. Once we're aware of these negative aspects, we can start to reduce them. This starts to make obvious sense once you've thought about it. A lot of nice words or behaviours are needed to undo the effects of a few hurtful ones.

Chapter 4 looks at some good habits or patterns that will help to reduce these bad habits or patterns. Good habits don't necessarily make a marriage happier, but they will make it last. Attitude is a good place to start. Your decision to love your spouse, no matter what, means that you are much less reliant on your spouse's behaviour or your feelings. Practical communication and problem-solving skills can also help deal with difficult issues. All of these are easy to learn.

Chapter 5 covers a few nifty tricks that you can keep up your sleeve to break a communication deadlock and get a couple talking. I take you step by step through three ways of doing this. Essentially, all three tricks do much the same thing. They highlight areas of difference that enable us to understand one other better. I especially like the idea of "love languages". "Emotional needs" is also helpful. I conclude with a powerful visual game that is brilliant for unknotting especially difficult issues with remarkable speed and efficiency. Use it with care!

Chapter 6 talks about "inventories". These are long lists of statements, like a questionnaire or shopping list, that get a couple to talk through the subjects known to be relevant to married life. Inventories have revolutionised the field of marriage education in the last few years by making it incredibly easy for the ordinary couple to be an effective support couple. Support couples now have a new tool that needs minimal or no training. Inventories provide structure, relevance, simplicity and flexibility. Couples love them. Support couples love them. Best of all, inventories are so simple that it's virtually impossible to misuse them.

Chapter 7 brings together the skills and the inventory and looks at how supporting couples works in practice. I run you through the whole process, covering basic ground rules, what a typical session involves and why, how to use an inventory flexibly, and what happens when you've finished.

Chapter 8 looks at what to do when your couple come up with particular problems. Overwhelmingly, your biggest problem will be in knowing how to handle rows and miscommunication. This is well within the capability of the average couple to deal with, using the skills we talked about in previous chapters. I cover some of the typically tricky issues couples find difficult to resolve – sex and money in particular. And I look at what to do when you face difficult individual issues – most often involving mental health and well-being.

Whatever the problem, the most important thing is that you aren't afraid to admit *"I don't know what to do"*. Even the best-informed uncles and aunts don't know everything. What they do know is their limits, where to go for advice, and when to suggest that a couple head for the doctor or counsellor. Support couples are ordinary but well-informed uncles and aunts. We do not have to be and are not expected to be experts.

Chapter 9 concludes the first part of the book with some stories from real-life couples. Whatever I have to say about how valuable and easy being a support couple is, and how more or less any married couple can provide effective support given a decent tool and some basic skills, you're bound to have doubts and concerns. Kate and I had doubts and concerns when we started. The couples we have supported had doubts and concerns when *they* started. But the proof of the pudding is what people actually say after they've had a go. Couples tell me again and again how much they enjoyed it. It wasn't scary. It wasn't intrusive. It wasn't threatening. It was encouraging. It was helpful. It was fun.

Part Two is written to give you some background information and answer questions you may have. Is marriage such a big deal? Do these skills really make a difference? Do support couples really make a difference? Shouldn't we leave all this to the professionals? Why do I feel so inadequate? This part is intended as a resource that you can dip into if you need extra information. It's a bit more technical, but I hope it should be an easy enough read for most people.

In Chapter 10, I look at how marriage differs from its alternatives in terms of how people behave and perform in life. The research is particularly clear that getting and staying married is good for our happiness, health and wealth, and that it helps us to live longer. People used to be able to claim that this is just because the people who marry start out better off. Research since the 1990s now shows this is only partly true at best, and quite false at worst. We can therefore start off with confidence that marriage is not some outdated religious idea. Marriage may not be perfect, but it remains the best way to live together and raise children as a family.

Chapter 11 looks at whether you can learn how to "do" marriage and relationships better. What is remarkable is that the key processes involved in marriage can be spotted at an early stage and used to predict the state of relationships years later with astonishing accuracy. That means we can be really certain what's important, rather than assuming what's important. These processes can be taught and tested to see if marriage education courses make marriages better. They do.

There are unanswered questions, though. Only a few courses have so far shown that they reduce divorce rates. So it's not yet clear whether other courses are effective. This could be a research problem rather than a course problem. But the fact that marriage-boosting and divorce-reducing courses exist shows that great marriage can be taught effectively.

In Chapter 12, I contrast being a support couple with couple counselling. Much of what we think about helping marriages comes from what we have been conditioned to think as counselling has become a familiar norm. This is an important point to make, because being a support couple is so different from couple counselling. I will present evidence for why couple counselling is often based on flawed principles that are unwanted, inappropriate and ineffective. In contrast, support couples offer the key principles of values, learning and support that are needed and effective. If you happen to be a couple counsellor, I hope you will consider the evidence I present with an open mind.

I finish with three Appendices. Since the reality is that many or even most support couples happen to be Christians, Appendix A looks at the Christian principles at work in this book. I didn't want to overplay these in the main text because

I believe that any married couple can be a support couple, regardless of belief. Appendix B offers a simple aide memoire summarising some key ideas to put into practice. Appendix C gives contact details for the inventory providers mentioned in the book.

So now it's up to you!

When Kate and I got married, it never occurred to us that we could learn about marriage or that we might have problems. Most couples today think like we did. Relationships are natural, aren't they? Persuading the invincible and in-love young couple to come and learn marriage skills is an uphill task.

But there is reason for hope. Unfamiliar but sensible ideas do become popular and normal with time. Once upon a time, learning how to breathe during childbirth must have seemed a ridiculous idea. After all, it's natural, isn't it? But perseverance and positive feedback have now made antenatal classes popular and normal. Some way behind these as regards social acceptability come breastfeeding classes. These will soon become the established custom. Parenting classes are becoming more widespread, if not yet the social norm. Right at the beginning of their journey towards social acceptability are relationship classes and support.

In the past, family life was indeed natural. We didn't need to learn it because our extended families provided our major natural source of values, learning and support. We learned it without even realising it. But as we lose extended family, so we lose our natural abilities to do family life well.

People are beginning to discover that it is OK to learn these things from others. Learning sensible principles strikes a chord with us because we want to do family life well. As we enjoy and benefit from the experience, we tell our friends. Ante-natal classes have become the accepted practice. In time, relationship education and support will also become normal.

This book will set you on the road to becoming a good enough support couple.

All you need to know is:

- That you don't need to be an expert or have a perfect marriage
- That using an inventory makes being a support couple and mentoring easy
- How to draw attention to bad habits
- How to affirm and reinforce good habits
- How to use some party tricks to break deadlocks
- To stay within your limitations
- To be flexible.

Further resources

So read Part One, get hold of a recognised inventory (see Chapter 6 and Appendix C), and you can become a support couple immediately! If you don't have a couple or need further resources, here are some other avenues to pursue.

In the UK, contact the NACFT at www.nacft.org.uk. Here you will find a list of local Community Family Trusts that use support couples. There is even a superb on-line manual explaining how to start a project near you!

Your contribution as a support couple will also be very welcome to Nicky and Sila Lee at www.themarriagecourse.org as part of their excellent pre-marriage course. Either of these approaches will plug you into an exciting new initiative called the National Couple Support Network.

Dave and Liz Percival's web site www.2-in-2-1.co.uk is a fantastic resource providing a comprehensive mine of information on UK courses, research and more or less anything you could want to know about relationship education. You can also subscribe to a weekly e-mail that will keep you up to date with marriage news. My own web site may also have a few things to interest you, at www.bcft.co.uk.

In the US, support couples are more commonly referred to as "mentor couples". Diane Sollee's www.smartmarriages.com provides a comprehensive listing of US marriage organisations, programmes and other information. Subscription to an e-mail list is available if you want to keep up to date. Diane runs a brilliant annual conference in the summer, which I highly recommend. Mike McManus at www.marriagesavers.org can put you in touch with a local mentor organisation.

In Australia, you can find conferences and resources at www.csme.catholic.au as well as subscribe to *Threshold*, the best magazine I've yet come across on marriage education. www.aifs.gov.au provides access to a huge amount of information for those interested in background research.

You may not believe me yet. But once you've had a go, you'll agree that being a support couple really is as straightforward as I say it is. All you need to do is have a go. You can e-mail me at info@bcft.co.uk to let me know how you get on.

Together we can start the enormous task of turning back the tide of family breakdown and rebuilding family stability. God bless.

Part One

Chapter 2 **Getting started**

In this chapter

- How almost any ordinary married couple can be a support/mentor couple
- Our first experience of being a support couple
- Three relationship patterns that anybody can learn to spot

Wanted: Ordinary couples

Supporting marriage is a job for ordinary couples. This very ordinariness can be a hard idea to accept. Yet if you've been married a few years and had your share of ups and downs, if you believe that other peoples' marriages matter, if you can sit down with a couple and talk about marriage – both theirs and yours – then you can be a good enough support couple. That's all. No other qualifications are needed. If you can learn a few practical skills on top, you can be a truly excellent support couple.

In particular, you don't need to have a perfect marriage. People who come across as too good to be true are usually exactly that. You need to have a good enough marriage that is sometimes joyful and exhilarating, sometimes mundane and workaday, and sometimes downright disappointing and painful. You're still married and you've survived. Your story acts as a powerful reminder to younger couples that marriage is not always a bed of roses. And when it's not, you don't have to give up.

Nor do you need to have any special expertise. Over the years, we've been conditioned to think about marriage in terms of *"guidance"*, *"counselling"*, *"therapy"*, *"help"* and *"problems"*. This not only creates a barrier for those who might like to talk and learn about marriage, it also creates the illusion that you have to be a trained expert. You don't.

I try to think about being a support couple in terms of extended family and education. Support couples are just like well-informed uncles and aunts. Being an uncle and aunt means you don't have to know all the answers. Being well informed means you know how to host an evening together and work through the process.

Don't allow the experts to tell you how well qualified you need to be. You don't. Nor should you pay attention to the little voice that questions how much you have to offer. If you needed to be an expert, your expertise would matter. But you don't, and it doesn't. The simple fact that you give your time, your hospitality, your interest and your care to another couple you barely know sends a huge message that their marriage is important.

You can be a support couple and make a difference. As a bonus, you'll even find the experience will help you focus on and strengthen your own marriage. Don't knock it until you've tried it!

Our first couple

Peter and Sally (names changed) were our very first couple. They had been put in touch with us soon after we had persuaded the pastor of our church that we should take over responsibility for marriage preparation classes. We had never done any kind of couple-to-couple work. But we had some experience of running weekend courses for already-married couples.

We had heard that mentoring, as it is commonly called in the US, seemed to be having remarkable success at reducing divorce rates in some American churches. The idea of sharing our experience of the ups and downs of married life with couples starting out made huge sense to us. Not only did we want others to benefit from some of the things we had learned, but we also wanted them to avoid the rubbish we'd been through in our marriage! You don't need to stare into the abyss to find out there are better options.

The fact we were in a church really wasn't the point. It certainly helped that our church had a supply of young couples getting married. But we wanted our programme to be a relationship programme rather than a church programme. We wanted it to be helpful, enjoyable and appropriate for any couple, regardless of their background. So we needed to have a go at mentoring in order to work out how best to train other married couples.

Peter and Sally called us to say they were due to get married in six months' time. First of all I invited them to come round for an hour or so to go through a questionnaire with a long list of statements. All they had to do was fill in an answer sheet saying whether they agreed or disagreed with each statement. This they did separately in two different rooms. No conferring!

The questionnaire took them both half an hour to complete. Afterwards there were a few nervous laughs about some of the more obscure questions. But the questionnaire had raised some interesting issues for them both. We made a date to have them round for dinner ten days later and encouraged them to talk as much as possible about the issues that had cropped up.

Our first evening together was wonderful. Frankly, Kate and I started off feeling a bit nervous because we hadn't done anything like this before. Teaching a group of couples from the safety of a platform was one thing. Having to interact with just one couple face to face was quite another. I was trying to play it cool and be encouraging. Kate was the brilliant hostess that she always is.

In fact, the whole support-couple thing couldn't have been easier. The hardest part of the evening was dispatching our children to bed in time so that we were ready for dinner at 8 o'clock. Putting our children to bed is a little like trying to complete a jigsaw puzzle that doesn't quite fit. You push one bit down and another bit pops up. You get one child into bed and another one pops back up. *"Just go to bed"* becomes our frustrated shout at all of the children at the tops of our voices. Compared to parenting, being a support couple is a piece of cake!

We started the evening over an informal dinner and a bottle of wine. We chatted about their backgrounds. Peter was from New Zealand; Sally was English. After meeting each other on holiday, they had built their relationship long distance by e-mail. Further holiday visits across the globe had cemented the love affair and they got engaged. Needless to say, the biggest issue taxing them was how to decide where to live. But this had also forced them to think more carefully than other couples about their long-term future. A good sign.

One other potential problem cropped up over dinner. Peter's parents were still married, whereas Sally's had separated when she was a teenager. This gave us more common ground, because my parents had split when I was three. Peter and Kate agreed that Sally and I sometimes behaved very oddly as a result. This prompted much laughter, although it was a serious matter that we talked about many times subsequently.

Kate and I sat opposite them with their answer sheets. We had sent off their original answers in the post for processing and their answers had come back to us neatly reorganised into subjects. The first subject was called *"Lifestyle Expectations"* – something to do with what each person imagines married life is supposed to be like. Their different childhood experiences were obviously going to play a big part in this.

For the next hour and a half, we got Peter and Sally to talk to each other about the questions in this section. I would get them to read out a question. *"Question 6: We have discussed our husband and wife roles."* From their answer sheet, I could then tell them how they had answered originally. *"Peter, you agreed. Sally, you disagreed."* They then talked about what they thought or felt about their answers.

"Are there any non-negotiables?" asked Kate. *"In other words, are there any roles you absolutely insist on either doing or not doing?"* Although there weren't any, I was mightily impressed with Kate's insightful question! She had found it among the suggested list of follow-up questions in front of her.

Throughout this part of the evening, I was very conscious that we had a lot of questions to get through and not very much time. So I was quite keen to try and move them along. This was difficult, because Peter and Sally were so enjoying talking things through. By the end, we had only finished the first dozen or so questions that made up the subject of "Lifestyle Expectations". Since the questionnaire had a dozen more subjects to cover, I wondered how we were going to cope without spending a dozen more evenings.

As it turned out, a lot of the questions we covered in subsequent evenings had already come up on our first night. This enabled us to work more quickly through two or three subjects each evening. Altogether, we spent four weekly evenings with Peter and Sally. So we didn't cover the entire questionnaire. But we did get through the subjects they thought needed to be addressed. For example, Sally talked for the first time about a particular habit of Peter's that drove her to distraction!

Many couples are like Peter and Sally. Their attitude towards each other helps them deal sensibly and lovingly with potential blockbuster issues – in their case, different countries and family backgrounds. Or they simply don't have huge issues that are difficult to reconcile. Other couples may have fewer differences but not be so positive towards each other.

Support couples don't have to solve problems. They just have to make sure problems are raised and aired. Simply by talking through their backgrounds and future plans, and the things they loved about each other as well as the things that made them different, Peter and Sally left oozing with confidence that *"Hey, we really are OK together!"* Job done.

This is what Sally told me some months later:

Looking back we realise how fortunate we were to have gone through the course, to have a safe space to think about all aspects of our relationship and to have had such support. We went into our marriage understanding what we were entering into. The course was great fun. It was such a laugh!

All that Kate and I had done was get them to talk about matters that were relevant to them. We hadn't solved anything for them. We hadn't given them advice or our opinions. We really hadn't been experts or counsellors. Having a list of questions to work through took away any worry about what to do with each evening. Having the follow-up questions made it very easy to get them to dig a bit deeper when it seemed necessary.

During dinner, we told them about our own marriage background. During the question times, we told them how we'd handled things when we got married. I think that hearing us talk about the not-so-good times encouraged them to be more open about their own difficult issues. We also tried to encourage them a lot. It wasn't difficult in their case because they were so good together. But even when you know you're good together, it's very reassuring to hear it from someone else.

After four evenings with us, Peter and Sally ended up knowing a bit more about each other as well as a great deal about the Bensons, warts and all! Four years later, they are still married. They are very happy and secure, despite going through some extremely taxing problems with moving home and country and having a baby. And they are still sufficiently friendly with us that they have helped look after our children twice in the last few months while Kate and I took a couple of short breaks away together. I guess we did OK.

Looking for patterns

Spending a few evenings walking your couple through a questionnaire and occasionally telling your story will make you a good enough support couple. Don't underestimate the benefit of giving them your time, your hospitality, your encouragement and your story. However inadequate you feel, the extraordinariness of what you offer is powerful stuff. After all, when did complete strangers or even acquaintances last provide you with several evenings of their time as well as their hospitality and friendly encouragement? Just doing these ordinary things will make your couple feel valued. Their marriage is worth the time you spend. At the very least they will be curious to know why you're doing it.

The big difference between a good enough support couple

and a truly excellent support couple is knowing how to identify and point out patterns of behaviour. You may not consider you have the experience or courage to do this on your
first evening. But as your experience grows, so will your confidence. Spotting patterns is really not that hard. None of
them are terribly difficult to understand. Learning how to
point them out is probably the harder part.

To get you started, I'm going to cover three tricks that
should be enough for handling most situations. You can dip
in and out of the later chapters to learn about these and other
skills in more detail. So, at risk of saying things twice, here is
the simple version of how to spot patterns.

Trick 1: STOP signs

The things we do to hurt one another have a bigger effect on
our relationship than the nice things we do or say. Everybody
instinctively knows when they feel hurt. I know when Kate
hurts me and Kate knows when I hurt her. Most of the time,
it happens automatically. We don't deliberately hurt each
other. They're bad habits that we don't even think about.

If you can label these bad habits and know what they
look like, it should become much easier to stop doing them.
You become aware of how you hurt one another. STOP signs
are what I call the four bad habits you need to recognise in
yourself first. Then you can help your couple recognise them
in their own behaviour. Think of STOP signs as bugs that are
there to be squashed. Bugs are not your fault or my fault.
They are bugs messing with our relationship and they need to
be stopped.

The first STOP sign is **S = Scoring points**: *"You did this."*
"Well you did that." This is not a healthy, co-operative conversation. It's a competition to see who wins. Normally, it's a bit
like a table tennis game. Occasionally it can escalate out of

control. *"You left the cap off the toothpaste." "Well you're not so perfect." "If you don't like it, then leave."* The game escalates from table tennis to tennis to warfare.

The second STOP sign is **T = Thinking the worst**: *"He's being nice. What does he want?"* or *"She forgot the cereal I asked for. She doesn't love me"* or *"He bought flowers. What's he done wrong?"* or *"She's doing it just to annoy me."* Something happens and we assume the worst. Yet being negative is almost never the deliberate intent. Thinking the worst is due to a faulty belief. Explanations are rarely sufficient to change these negative assumptions.

The third STOP sign is **O = Opting out**: *"I give up... I just can't win with you... I'm not taking this any more... I'm off to the pub."* Opting out is where one or both people withdraw in the face of a difficult issue. It could be emotional or physical withdrawal. Men tend to opt out more often because they think women are nagging and causing conflict. In reality, women are usually just trying to talk something over. Having opted out of an argument over money, for example, money becomes more difficult to discuss next time. Opting out is so destructive precisely because issues are shut down one by one until there is nothing left to discuss. Then the couple get a divorce, claiming to have grown apart. Taking time out to calm down is not the same as opting out. It's OK to take a breather to calm down, as long as you return to discuss the problem.

The fourth STOP sign is **P = Putting down**: You can put somebody down in a number of ways, starting with character assassination: *"You moron...you're useless"* to the more subtle *"You shouldn't think like that...don't worry...don't be sad."* Rolling eyes and clicking tongues have a similarly destructive effect. All of these things put others down and invalidate them.

Learning to recognise these STOP signs in our own marriage is a good starting point. I don't think I score points or put Kate down too much when we argue. But I do tend to think the worst and opt out. I assume I'm in trouble with Kate unless proven otherwise. In reality, Kate tells me that I'm not in trouble nearly as much as I think. Alas it's something I have to live with. No amount of talk convinces me to stop thinking the worst. I also tend to hide away from Kate and the kids more than I should. I opt out because it's safer for me to sit behind my computer screen than to do the difficult stuff of relating face to face. The presence of these automatic STOP signs is bound to reflect my family background. I could lie back and accept this as inevitable and unchangeable. Or I can recognise my bad habits and try to learn better ways of doing things.

Pointing out STOP signs gently but clearly is a huge gift to a couple. *"Guys, that sounds like a put-down to me."* *"Which STOP sign do you think is in play here?"* It may feel risky for you to point these things out. But the seeds of future destruction are otherwise being sown with these bad habits. Left unchecked, STOP signs will deepen and grow and consume the marriage over time.

Researchers say these automatic bad habits are the single most important factor in the early years of marriage. STOP signs are easy enough to remember. I discuss them in more detail in Chapter 3. Now you know what they look like, you can start cutting them out of your own marriage and helping others to do the same. Easy.

Trick 2: Listening

Everybody instinctively knows when somebody isn't listening to them. They may not know *how* they know, but they know. When Kate says to me, *"You're not listening, are you?"* she's always right. I can pretend I heard. I repeat what she said. But she knows. Everybody plays this game.

The main way she knows I'm not listening is through eye contact. You can't be really sure someone is listening when they are looking away from you. They might be distracted by what they are looking at. They might be thinking what to say next. What is very unlikely is that they have both heard and understood what you said. Their mind is elsewhere.

Another way she knows I'm not listening is the way I reply. Instead of acknowledging what Kate said, I change the subject. For example, Kate says, *"I'm worried about my friend."* I might reply, *"Oh, she'll be alright."* In this case I overlooked Kate's feeling and replied about the fact. I almost certainly would have been looking away while Kate was speaking in order to prepare my reply.

So when you notice that your couple are talking to each other but not really engaging fully with good eye contact, the chances are that they are not listening. For example, when he looks away halfway through listening to what she's saying, he is probably thinking what to say next rather than listening. His reply will confirm whether this is true. If he changes the subject, he hasn't listened to her. Of course it's not only men who don't listen…

If you're watching how your couple make eye contact during conversation, you will start to spot the pattern. Most of the time, it really doesn't matter that people communicate in this way. It's hugely normal to be thinking what to say next instead of listening. But when something really important crops up, such as *"I felt really upset with the way you spoke to me the other day"*, poor listening can turn a simple frustration into a major row quite quickly. *"See. He just doesn't understand me!"*

As good support couples, you should pay attention to the

way each of your couple uses eye contact to show they're paying attention and listening. When the big misunderstanding takes place, you can be very direct as well as gentle. *"Guys, just stop there a second. I'm not sure Sally quite heard what Peter was saying and it sounded important to me. Peter, please tell Sally again what you just said. Sally, tell Peter what he just said but use your own words. Is that OK? Off you go..."*

In this way, you can get them to check with each other that what she heard was indeed what he meant, or vice versa. You may have to try it several times. Use your hands to direct operations if you need. This is a skill variously called Paraphrasing or Active Listening or Speaker/Listener. You can read more about it in Chapter 4. Hopefully, this should improve their understanding a great deal on difficult issues. All you've done is spot that they needed to communicate better. And you did it just by watching their eyes. Easy.

Trick 3: Love languages

All of us think we know what love is. Yet the very fact that so many books are written on the subject of love suggests that it might be open to interpretations other than our own.

Kate and I have very different interpretations of love. I show my love to Kate by giving her hugs and by doing the washing up for her. What I really like her to do is hug me and do things for me, such as cook me dinner. I feel really blessed and appreciative when she does these things.

The problem is that this is not at all how Kate views love. She shows her love to me by wanting to chat. More than anything, she loves hanging out with me or her friends and chatting. Nothing could make her happier than a couple of hours spent chewing the cud. When I chat to her, she feels really blessed and appreciative.

What this suggests is that, for Harry, the languages of

love are TOUCH and ACTIONS. For Kate, the languages of love are TIME and WORDS. Because we are so different, we don't naturally feed love to each other in the way it is best received.

Until we recognise this simple idea, love can seem an extremely confusing business. Let's say I sidle up to Kate and wrap my arms around her. *"Get off,"* she says, pushing me away. She feels imposed upon because what she really wanted was for me to sit down and talk through her day. I feel rejected and wary of making loving advances next time.

The problem is that we automatically assume everybody else receives love from us in the same way we like giving love. After all, that's how it works for me!

There are supposedly five love languages – TIME, WORDS, ACTIONS, GIFTS and TOUCH. TIME means I want us to hang out together. WORDS means I want us to talk together. ACTIONS means I want us to do things either together or for each other. GIFTS means I want us to give thoughtful presents to each other. TOUCH means I want us to hug and hold hands together.

As with STOP signs, love language is a tremendously simple and powerful idea to explain, learn and apply both for your own marriage and also for your couple. There's more on this in Chapter 5. As soon as the idea is discussed, it will prompt a great deal of discussion around the table. The key to finding out anybody's love language is to ask how they love their friends. The key to applying this to your loved one is to ask whether you have got it right. After all, they are the expert on their own love language. So it's best to check. Easy.

An example of how to point out patterns

Pointing out a pattern may still seem an unnerving prospect. But it's really important that you do it. Your couple won't thank you for taking the easy route and not saying anything. Let me tell you a story to show how easy it can be.

Recently, I was running a two-day relationships course for inmates and their partners in Bristol prison. One of the couples comprised a young mum and her boyfriend. To put it mildly, this girl's personal history was somewhat exotic. She had three young children, all from previous relationships. Yet she was unable to see them because she'd been "sectioned". The government had decided she was not fit to parent her own children because of her poor mental health. Needless to say, she was a punchy character, although also amusing to chat with.

During the lunch break on the first day of the course, her boyfriend went off to make her a cup of coffee. *"It'll taste of gnat's piss,"* she said dismissively. I smiled at her, *"And which STOP sign would that be?"* She thought for a second and said, *"Oh, it's a put-down."* We continued chatting about her home life and her relationship. When her man returned, she grinned and nodded in his direction. *"He's a nightmare,"* she said. I smiled again, *"So which STOP sign is that, then?"* She was quicker this time. We both laughed. Her put-downs were in no way malevolent. But put-downs they were, nonetheless.

A week later, we returned to the prison for the second day of the course. I started by asking what anyone had got out of the course last week. The girl's hand shot up. Remembering her background situation, I was intrigued to hear what had happened. *"I remember the STOP signs, especially put-downs,"* she said. *"And I've really noticed how I tend to put people down without even realising I'm doing it. This week, my mum told me how much nicer I've been to be around."*

I'm still really chuffed about this. It's one of the small victories I live by. All I had done was risk the embarrassment of asking which STOP sign she thought she was using. Because

I asked her with a big grin on my face and the right attitude, she didn't find the question remotely offensive. Because I asked her at all, she had made the connection in her mind between what she had been taught and how she actually behaved. It was only a little thing that I did. It wasn't hard to point out the pattern. It wasn't scary. But it just might make all the difference to her relationships from now on.

Getting started

I hope that what I've written in this chapter gives you enough to think *"Yes, we could do that!"* After all, spending a few evenings with a couple while you walk them subject by subject through a questionnaire is really not very difficult. They get to do the work, not you. They are the experts, not you. The vast majority of young couples find this a huge confidence-boosting exercise. How else are they to be really sure that they are good for each other? It's normal to have doubts and worries, even if they are kept firmly in check. Covering the major issues means there are no hidden surprises. They feel affirmed and confident. You give them that.

Sharing stories about the ups and downs of your own marriage is also really not very difficult. It may feel a little unusual and even scary if you haven't talked to another couple about your marriage before. But you are showing them another marriage close up. It shows them how they don't have to be happy every minute of every day. They can survive the inevitable bad times and yet still grow closer in love together over time. You show them that.

The practical skills that take you from being a good enough support couple to a truly excellent one involve spotting and pointing out patterns. If you can identify STOP signs in the way they behave towards each other, you're halfway towards reducing the ways they hurt each other. If you can observe the way they make eye contact, you're halfway towards helping them communicate better. If you can work out your own love languages, you're halfway to helping them find new ways of showing love to each other.

All you need to complete the task is to take the risk of pointing these things out. By reducing their STOP signs, they have so much less chance of wrecking their relationship. By listening with their eyes and paraphrasing, they will understand each other so much better. By knowing how to put their love languages into practice, they have so much more chance of deepening their relationship and keeping it that way.

To get started, all you need is what you've read so far. Of course you'll want to learn a bit more about certain things – how the inventory works, how certain skills work. The remaining chapters cover this in much more detail. Dip in and out of them as you see fit. You may be content to stick to the simple descriptions. You may want to know more after you've got started. Or you may want to know the entire rationale in detail. It's all here if you want it.

Remember that you don't have to be an expert and you don't have to have a perfect marriage. So you can relax. They do the work, not you. Think of yourself as a well-informed uncle and aunt. Then you don't have to know any clever answers or pretend to be anything that you're not. Just being friendly hosts, being real about your own ups and downs and helping them through the questionnaire will make you a good enough support couple or mentor. But if you can keep your eyes open and learn how to spot and point out simple patterns, you can be a truly excellent support couple or mentor.

Chapter 3   **Bad habits**

In this chapter

- Four STOP signs to watch out for
- Interference that messes with our communication
- Myths that make us self-centred

The importance of spotting patterns

One of the biggest gifts a support couple can give a younger couple is to point out patterns of behaviour, both positive and negative. All couples have patterns of behaviour. The more positive patterns we have – good habits – the happier we're likely to be. The fewer negative patterns we have – bad habits – the more likely we are to stay together. Because these habits become so ingrained in a relationship, they can be hard to spot from the inside. But they are much easier for outsiders to identify.

Spotting both good and bad habits and gently pointing them out is perhaps your most important role. Pointing out good habits is really encouraging to a young couple starting out. It reminds them and reassures them that they are good for each other. In a world where lifelong marriage is increasingly under threat, it helps to dispel their doubts and build their confidence in their future together. Pointing out bad habits is also really valuable to them. By illuminating unhealthy behaviours in their relationship, it raises their awareness and gives them increased choice. They then have the opportunity to leave things as they are or take action. Time spent with a support couple may be the first time that anybody has been specific either in affirming their positive behaviours or in cautioning them about negative behaviours.

How to destroy a perfectly good relationship

In general, our good habits of behaviour towards one another matter far less than our bad habits. It is the subtle but destructive automatic behaviours that eat away at a relationship over time. As bad habits become more strongly established, they become hard to break. Soon whole areas of the relationship become no-go areas and eventually the marriage falls apart.

To demonstrate the truth of this, think for a moment of the ridiculous old saying that says *"Sticks and stones can break my bones but words can never hurt me"*. It's ridiculous because physical wounds heal relatively quickly, whereas the emotional scars of words can devastate and last. It can take only the tiniest negative word or action from a spouse or a close friend or relative to close you down. It could be a sharp comment, raised eyes, a turned back, a dismissive air, or simply your perception that things are bad. Whatever it is, when you feel hurt, you are much more likely to be suspicious about any subsequent positive behaviours.

So if you've ever wanted to know how to destroy a perfectly good relationship, pay attention to this chapter! I'll start with some especially virulent behaviours that will definitely point you in the direction of the divorce courts. Most of us will recognise a few of these in our own relationships if we're honest. Then I'll show you how to ensure you get your wires well and truly crossed whenever you try to talk about anything. I'll finish with some of the most pervasive myths or destructive beliefs that can keep your marriage an unrealistic and impossible dream.

Behaving badly

Many researchers from the 1990s onwards have concluded that the most important factors in a marriage are the negative ways we relate to one another. I've written more on this in Chapter 11. Two particular groups in the US have produced a list of the four biggest no-nos that point towards divorce.

One group, led by Professor John Gottman, describes how *Criticism* can lead to *Contempt*, which in turn leads to *Defensiveness* and finally *Withdrawal*. The other group, led by Professors Howard Markman and Scott Stanley of the PREP programme, describe *Withdrawal*, *Invalidation*, *Negative Interpretation* and *Escalation*.

It shouldn't be too surprising to find that the two lists have a lot in common. Ultimately, both reflect our attitudes. I've revamped these patterns of behaviour as STOP signs, which we covered briefly in the last chapter, to make them easier to remember and act upon. Let me now describe what these look like in a bit more detail.

STOP sign 1: S = Scoring points

Scoring points usually sounds like this: *"You did this."* *"Well you did that."* Each of us has our finger in the other person's chest, blaming, accusing, scoring points. *"You..."*

This can begin to sound like a game of table tennis. Harry is at one end and Kate at the other. I start off by batting the ball to Kate, using my table-tennis bat. She knocks it back at me. I knock it back at her. And so on. At some stage she hits the ball back to me just that little bit harder. I start to feel both miffed and competitive. As the ball reaches me I quickly exchange my table-tennis bat for a tennis racket. I can then belt the ball back, hoping it will get past her defences. Of course it doesn't, because she has brought out her own tennis racket. The game becomes more of a slugging match. Eventually one of us pulls out the Challenger tank we keep in reserve and fires the ping-pong ball back from the barrel with such velocity that it wipes out our opponent. Game over. Oops...

I started off having a disagreement with my wife. It all seemed pretty harmless at first as we exchanged friendly banter. Next thing I know we have become competitors and opponents. I am out not just to win but to destroy her.

That's the extreme version of scoring points. The everyday version seldom gets much further than table-tennis bats. Instead of working together as a team, we are trying to score points by changing the subject. *"You didn't empty the bin today."* *"Well, hang on a second. You didn't do the ironing like you said you would."*

Those familiar with Prime Minister's Question Time in the British parliament will recognise a perfect example of two people scoring points. The two political leaders face each other across the floor of parliament playing verbal table tennis, never really engaging with one issue, always retaliating or point-scoring. Eventually both sit down after their encounter. Neither ends up the richer for it. Nobody ever wins because the subject is always changed. Both end up bruised, angry and withdrawn.

Scoring points is bad news. Don't do it!

STOP sign 2: T = Thinking the worst

Imagine that some event takes place or someone says something that is either completely harmless or even quite positive. When you take it in the worst possible way, you are thinking the worst. This is also called a "negative interpretation". Let's see some examples.

Imagine that one day I bring home flowers for my wife, Kate. She could respond by thinking the best, being really grateful and appreciative, and saying thank you – which is probably the way Kate really would respond. The rest of the evening would most likely go very well indeed. Now imagine instead that she's had a bad time recently and is feeling hurt. She could look at the flowers, think the worst, be suspicious, and wonder what I've done wrong. That is very definitely a negative way of interpreting things! I would have to work hard to avoid putting a foot wrong and make the rest of the evening go well.

Imagine another scene in the kitchen. I am chatting to Kate while she is making a cup of coffee. To my slight amazement, I notice that she's only made the single cup for herself. There's no coffee for me. Yet here I am. I'm her husband. I'm not a bad bloke. Yet she's left me out. I could react in two main ways. I could think the best and assume that she's simply forgotten. It may simply be that she's been operating on automatic while we've been talking. She has probably got a million other things on her mind. Yet I could also think the worst and view it negatively. She didn't make me coffee deliberately. It's a snub. We had a row several days ago and she's still cross with me. Worse, it could be that she doesn't love me. I wonder if she did it on purpose?

Both examples take place entirely in the mind. They are based on some deeply-held assumptions – *"He's done something wrong"*; *"She doesn't love me"* – that are quite hard to test and refute. Whatever I say about the flowers, she won't believe me. Whatever she says about the coffee, I won't believe her. What's worst about thinking the worst is that our behaviour is likely to deteriorate as a result.

Thinking the worst is the automatic assumption that some negative relationship experience or pattern of behaviour from the past also applies right now. Thinking the worst happens to be my own biggest personal problem. Unless I have recently seen some hard evidence of connection from Kate, I assume I'm in trouble. I have no idea why I assume I'm in trouble all the time. But it leads me to behave defensively. If Kate tells me something needs doing, I'm more likely to feel defensive and may even snap back at her or ignore her. This is not great for our marriage. We then spiral downwards as Kate gets cross because I withdraw and get grouchy. This then confirms that I need to withdraw further.

Thinking the worst is bad news. Don't do it!

STOP sign 3: O = Opting out

You may have read John Gray's book *Men are from Mars, Women are from Venus*. He's made a lot of money from the simple observation that, on the whole, men and women are different. Men and women think differently and behave differently. My own observation is that those who enjoy his books tend to fit such a generalisation or stereotype. But a significant minority does not fit that stereotype. Since my wife, Kate, and I fit the stereotype pretty well in this case, I'll tell you how we deal with problems.

Kate tells me that women typically like talking about their problems out loud until the problems have been aired enough to go away. Women are therefore external processors of problems. Their main goals are to express their feelings and to build the relationship. The problem itself is not necessarily the big deal. As a man, I find this hard to understand.

I, on the other hand, as a man, typically see a problem as something to be solved...once. I don't want to hear endlessly about a problem. Once is quite enough. I've heard it. I've probably solved it in my head or logged that it needs dealing with. Men are therefore internal processors of problems. When I hear it again, my mind starts to wander. The third time begins to feel like nagging. *"Look, I heard you the first time,"* I might say.

At this point various options arise. I might simply switch off. I might get cross. I might feel defensive. I might feel prickly. But because the problem has kept coming back at me, even when I've said I'd deal with it or I've solved it in my mind, it begins to seem like conflict. I don't care for conflict in the home. Conflict normally means I get to use my supply of testosterone. That's a job for outside the home, not inside. Time to opt out and withdraw.

Opting out or withdrawal can mean a number of things. I might look away. I might simply stop listening. I might even get up and leave the room. Because I'm naturally introverted, withdrawal to me represents safety. I can find it threatening being with people. In many ways I like and prefer being on my own. Unfortunately, when I withdraw to that place of safety, Kate is starting to think, *"He doesn't care"*. That's how opting out looks to her. Kate's an extrovert. She enjoys being around people. Talking about a problem is her way of connecting. I can see that as conflict, from which I need to escape. I think she's nagging. She thinks I don't care.

Of course, in the stereotype, what the wife is trying to do is connect and what the husband is trying to do is avoid conflict. They don't recognise that their loved one thinks differently. Although it's predominantly men who tend to opt out of arguments, in many situations and households it could easily be the wife, or both husband and wife, who withdraws. Either way, opting out is bad news. In fact, some researchers claim it's the number-one predictor of divorce. Every time you withdraw, you make it harder to be open to each other next time. Do that enough and pretty soon there's little to talk about. You drift apart. You lose your friendship. Presto! One of you files for divorce.

Opting out is bad news. Don't do it!

STOP sign 4: P = Putting down

Researchers call it "invalidation" when we put down or undermine one another. I might put you down because I'm feeling defensive, or angry, or hurt. Instead of focusing on the issue, I switch my attack to put you down as a person. Invariably, put-downs reflect an attitude of contempt for the other person.

Some put-downs are not so subtle. On the one hand there's outright character assassination: *"You stupid idiot." "You moron." "You're useless." "You're a prat."* Generalisations are especially wounding: *"You've never been any good."* These pay no attention to the matter at hand but simply condemn the person. Rolling your eyes and clicking your tongue have much the same effect. They suggest an attitude of contempt or dismissal.

On the other hand, there are more subtle ways to do each other down. The most common of these is to deny the validity of your spouse's thoughts or feelings. For example:

- *"I had a bad day at the office today. My boss blew me out."*
  "Well maybe you deserved it."

- *"I feel really angry about what the government are doing."*
  "You shouldn't. I'd have thought you have more important things to worry about at home."

A third way to put one another down is to overlook something that deserves positive comment. A cake that has been made specially is eaten without thanks. The clothes that have been cleaned are worn without comment. When I do something nice for you, it's reasonable to expect some sort of positive comment. When it doesn't happen, I may feel put down.

Put-downs are bad news. Don't do it!

STOP signs

These four STOP signs reflect a bad attitude. It's in the mind that bad behaviours begin. And it's in the mind that changes in behaviour will take place. When I have a bad attitude towards you, I'm not valuing you. You don't feel valued and so you react to me in a negative way. Our marriage spirals downhill. When I have a good attitude towards you, I am valuing you. You feel valued and react more positively. Our marriage spirals uphill. It's as simple as that.

If I score points with you, I'm more concerned about defending myself than about dealing with the matter that is of importance to you. With a more positive attitude, I'm less likely to feel defensive and change the subject. I'm more likely to be able to talk through your issue.

If I think the worst, I'm making some big assumptions about how you see me that are very likely to be wrong most of the time. Mostly, you're not out to get me. Mostly, you do the best you can. With a more positive attitude, I'm more likely to give you the benefit of the doubt, which is right most of the time. With a more positive air about the place, our marriage has a better chance.

If I opt out or withdraw, I'm more concerned about my own hurts and about defending myself than with finding out what's eating you and what's best for you. With a more positive attitude, I'd be more concerned to stick around to hear your story. I'd be less likely to take things personally.

If I put you down, I'm showing a disrespectful, critical and contemptuous attitude towards you. I've switched my focus off the issue and onto you the person. With a more positive attitude, I'd be less likely to attack you personally and more likely to discuss the issue.

Communicating badly

Whereas behaving badly mostly reflects a bad attitude, communicating badly mostly reflects a lack of knowledge or skills. Communicating well is something that can be learned. The problem for most of us is that, unless we've been brought up in a family who communicate really well, we may have little idea what great communication looks like.

Figure 3.1 highlights five main elements involved in com-

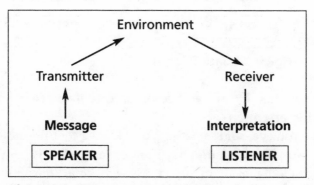

Figure 3.1 One-way communication

munication. The SPEAKER has a message, which is transmitted through the environment. The LISTENER receives the message and interprets it. It's so simple, what can possibly go wrong?

It may help to think about how soldiers communicate. As long as their radios are working, within range and tuned to the same frequency, communication takes place. Common language – like "Roger", "Over", "Out" – and procedures make it easy to understand one another. It's a system that works well and limits scope for error. That's good communication.

Back in the home, we don't have to worry about radios and frequencies. But because we don't have a common language or procedure, we have enormous scope for interference. As soon as we start thinking about this, it is amazing that men and women ever communicate successfully!

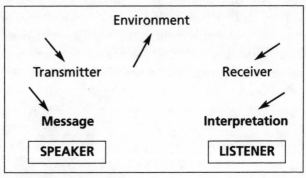

Figure 3.2 Interference

Interference 1: You can't communicate if you're not paying attention

Have you ever said something and known that the other person wasn't listening? The most obvious clue is that they weren't looking you in the eye. My wife, Kate, knows instantly when my mind has wandered off. *"You're not listening, are you?"* and both of us know it's true. But how many times have I repeated back what she said in order to cover my tracks? *"Of course I was listening. You said..."* I can repeat back brilliantly, word for word.

But of course Kate was right. She *knew* I hadn't listened. The two big clues were my lack of eye contact and my word-for-word repeating back. I don't know what it is about eye-to-eye contact but it seems incredibly important in communication. I don't know why we don't look at each other's ears or mouths to show we're listening. But we don't. We look at eyes, somehow connecting brain to brain.

Lack of eye contact is one reason why car journeys can be the worst times to discuss a contentious issue. Kate and I have had some of our most appalling rows in cars. We're excellent communicators. I teach it, after all. But without eye contact, I can't see her eyes and she can't see mine. In addition, I can't give her 100% attention when I'm focusing at least in part on driving. The end result is that neither of us can tell if we're really listening. Neither of us feels understood. A minor difference quickly escalates into a major row. Trying to withdraw after that is hard when you're stuck in a car together and can't get away.

So how come when I repeat back so accurately and brilliantly she doesn't believe me? The fact that I can do it is simple. In my brain is a short-term memory that stores information for a few seconds, just like an audio tape. All I have to do is play back the tape. Unfortunately, Kate – and probably the entire cunning female species – is wise to that too. The reason she knows I haven't listened is because I've repeated back word for word. Look back at the communication diagram (Figure 3.1) again. All I've shown her is that my receiver is working. What I didn't show her was that I'd interpreted what she said. She knew I wasn't listening.

Unless I can look into Kate's eyes, neither she nor I have any guarantee that I'm paying attention. She might tell me something from another room. She might talk to me when I'm looking at my computer screen or watching TV or reading the kids a story. She might talk to me when I'm driving. But in every single case, if she can't see my eyes looking at her eyes when she tells me something, she knows I'm not giving her my full attention.

I know now that when Kate has something to say, I need to turn away from what I'm doing and look her in the eye. Then both of us know for sure that I'm paying attention.

Interference 2: You can't communicate if you're wound up

Unfortunately, even if I turn round and look Kate in the eye, my mind may still be affected by something that has been going on. I may have had a bad day at work. Somebody may have said something that hurt me. I may be angry about something the kids have done or said. I could be concerned because we seem to be running short of cash this month. Even when I pay attention, my mind is deeply influenced by my feelings.

There is an acronym that helps put up a warning sign when emotions are running high. It's "HALT". If I'm H = Hungry, A = Angry, L = Lonely or T = Tired, I shouldn't try to communicate anything meaningful. I should HALT.

If I'm tired or angry, I can easily say something I didn't mean or mean something I didn't say. Any parent can recognise how easy it is to take out frustration from work on the children or frustration with the children on your wife or husband. Small mistakes are misinterpreted as deliberate. Minor imperfections or omissions are jumped on as careless.

The words I say and the words I hear are distorted as they pass through the foggy lens of hunger, anger, loneliness or tiredness. This is not good news. When we have something important to discuss and I am feeling Hungry, Angry, Lonely or Tired, I know I need to HALT and come back to the subject later.

Interference 3: You can't communicate if you don't know and accept each other's differences

Each of us has a different way of communicating the same thing. Even when I'm paying attention and not feeling wound up, important differences can scupper our communication. We may be able to overlook them in the good times when we're getting on well. But they can drive couples mad with rage when things aren't going so well. An example is how most women prefer to talk their problems through with others whereas most men prefer to think them through on their own.

There is a great variety of combinations of communication styles within couples. The problem comes either when Kate and I are unaware of these differences or when we simply refuse to acknowledge to ourselves that another way of doing things is equally valid. It's simply who I am and who you are. The mistake is to assume everyone is, or should be, like me. So being expressive and airy is OK. Being concise and punchy is OK too. They're just different.

One especially important difference within couples concerns how loudly you and I talk. If you were to stand anywhere near the Benson household for more than a few minutes, sooner or later you would hear shouting. We have six kids, and shouting is our familiar means of communicating. High volume is a way of getting the message through.

Imagine that somebody stays with us who has been brought up in a mouse-like household where everyone speaks softly. If they are used to people who talk quietly and peacefully in a civilised manner, it must seem like walking into Baghdad when the bombs are falling. For them, volume is used only when conflict occurs. The Bensons use volume, lots of it. Therefore the Bensons are at war. Of course, now that I've told you this, you won't notice when we really *are* at war...

The point of all this is that men and women have different styles of and beliefs about communication; not wrong, not right. It's just a good idea to acknowledge what those differences are and accept that it's OK to be different.

Destructive myths about marriage

I want to finish off by lifting the lid on a couple of destructive myths about marriage. These beliefs are so well embedded in our Western culture that we can laugh dismissively at them while at the same time falling prey to their destructive underlying assumptions.

The first lie is that *"they lived happily ever after"*. The second is that you should *"follow your heart"*. The problem with both myths is that they put the burden of success for our relationship squarely on the shoulders of the other person. The other person fits my image of perfection. The day I wake up aware of their faults, that's presumably it. Off to follow my heart to the next person and live happily ever after...for a while. What this is about is an absolution of responsibility. *"My part of the deal is to do X. Your part of the deal is to do Y. I'm going to sleep with you, marry you, etc., so long as you make me happy."* Marriage is not a contract. Marriage is a promise – for worse, for poorer, in sickness. It's hard to stick out the difficult times in a marriage when you're supposed to live happily ever after and follow your heart.

Myth 1: *"They lived happily ever after"*

In the Western world we have been brought up on harmless fairy tales. When you think about them, most contain half-witted notions of how relationships work in the real world. For example, stories like Cinderella are escapist and romantic. Yet Cinderella is perhaps the most obvious perpetrator of the myth *"they lived happily ever after"*. The escapist and romantic part of the story surrounds the girl who rises from rags to riches. Doubtless most of us born outside royal palaces can associate with such a character. The lure of a new life of wealth and comfort is part of what drives so many to play the lottery. Part of the lure is the dream of the perfect person – rich, charming and handsome.

Yet we rarely stop to think about whether the prince really is charming. As Cinderella runs off into the night, we learn that the charming prince hasn't bothered to find out the girl's name. The charming man can't even surge into action to chase after the girl as she disappears into the night. Our prince's one vaguely redeeming act is to send his minions out to find the owner of the discarded slipper. What inspired him to do it? Sex, presumably, since conversation doesn't appear to have featured too strongly. Eventually the girl is found because she has abnormally small feet. She is summoned to the palace and *"they lived happily ever after"*.

Would their marriage have survived? Who knows. Their relationship is initially based entirely on looks. Otherwise they are complete strangers, with little or nothing in common. Complete strangers can and do have very successful arranged marriages. But arranged marriages have tremendous social support and family backing. At the risk of being a party-pooper, I'd say the odds for an uncommunicative Cinderella and a love-struck prince don't look good. It would be hard to imagine what they could possibly have in common. Am I wrecking love? No. I'm just being realistic. He wants her body. She wants his wealth and status. Having achieved that, what's next? We're left in the dark.

The story of Sleeping Beauty is even more bizarre. The poor princess is fed a particularly powerful sleeping pill. A random man cuts down a hedge and marches into the sleepy, overgrown palace. He artfully ignores all the other bodies lying around the place and magically locates her bedroom. He bends down and kisses the cobwebbed sleeping girl. She wakes up and immediately spots a man worthy of her hand in marriage, presumably from his face alone. It's an unusual approach. But everyone else wakes up from their own reverie, shakes off their cobwebs, and is happy. The couple *"lived happily ever after"*.

How can I be so sceptical? Easy. We get this story in school books and Hollywood films. Every love story is notionally about romance but in reality about individual fulfilment. Every happy ending leaves us feeling good because we can presume eternal happiness. Happiness is always the key. But since happiness is a feeling that comes and goes, the likelihood is that the relationship or marriage will go the same way. Our secret dreams have been conditioned by endless repetition of this myth. We expect happiness. If I'm not happy, leave. The *"happily ever after"* myth is at the root of most adultery and most divorces.

Myth 2: *"Follow your heart"*

A few years ago, I remember going to see a film called *The English Patient*. I saw it again recently on video. It is a wonderful drama about heroic pioneers making maps of Africa during the war. The hero falls in love with the young wife of another pioneer. After the husband finds out the truth, he crashes his survey aeroplane into them in an attempt to kill all three. The wife is fatally injured and dies after the hero leaves to find help. The film tells the story of the man as he recalls the whole tragic experience from a bed, following his own subsequent crash. The film plays to our emotions so much that the foolishness of infidelity is almost overlooked. After all, the new love seems so romantic, so right and so much more wonderful. And it's wartime. Life is short and precious. She followed her heart.

In the cold light of day, away from the emotionally charged environment of the film, I remember wondering about the dubious morality of this story. The foolishness of the new wife in following her heart is astonishing. Both of the lovers behaved like idiots. He stole his best friend's new wife. She gave up a perfectly good marriage in a moment of madness. It never seemed likely that they could have ended up living happily ever after. There was always the problem of the abandoned husband and friend, who seemed a decent-enough bloke. There was also the problem that the new man would twig how easily his lover had abandoned her husband for sex and even more adventure. It would be only a matter of time before she abandoned him too at the drop of a hat. Insecurity and doubt would set in. Communication would be framed through this particular foggy lens of self-protection. The new relationship, or even the second marriage, would last ten minutes.

It's terribly tempting to believe we should follow our heart. After all, our satisfaction and happiness is everything. We feel good when we see people who are happy. We want to make things better when people are not happy. Yet in our rush to seek out instant gratification, our feelings can overpower our common sense. If I'm not happy, I should get a new job, new car, new marriage. Follow my heart – from job to job, car to car, house to house. Don't worry about the trail of devastation I leave behind. Changing relationships to follow your heart is a selfish and dud strategy. You will never be satisfied because nobody can meet your perfect expectations – and stay perfect. *"Follow your heart"*? No thanks.

Summary

One of the most important roles of a support couple is to spot patterns or habits, whether positive or negative, good or bad. The presence of good habits increases the odds of a happy marriage. But that doesn't mean the marriage will last. The presence of bad habits decreases the odds of a lasting marriage. But that doesn't mean a couple won't often be happy. We need to point out both – reinforce the good and raise awareness of the bad.

This chapter is full of really important information for anyone who wants marriages to succeed. We can be really confident that the formula for success depends very largely on the presence or otherwise of bad habits. Researchers have identified four especially destructive behaviours, or bad habits, that will eat away at a relationship. I've called them STOP signs.

S = Scoring points means I'm more concerned about my thoughts and feelings than yours.

T = Thinking the worst means I assume you're not concerned about my thoughts and feelings.

O = Opting out means I'm more concerned about my thoughts and feelings than yours.

P = Putting down means I'm not concerned about your thoughts and feelings.

The really good news about all of these is that it's my bad attitude at fault, not yours. In marriage it therefore takes one to tango. Just as I can destroy our marriage with my bad attitude, I can build our marriage with my good attitude.

While bad behaviour usually reflects my bad attitude, bad communication usually reflects my ignorance. Maybe it simply doesn't occur to me that I can't communicate well when I'm not paying attention. Maybe it simply doesn't occur to me that I can't communicate well when I'm emotionally wound up. HALT is a good way of remembering this – I shouldn't communicate when I'm H = Hungry, A = Angry, L = Lonely or T = Tired. Maybe it simply doesn't occur to me that you and I might have different styles and beliefs associated with the way we communicate. I know that now. You know that now. So there's no excuse. I'll tell you how to deal with these problems in the next chapter on good habits.

So we could trash our marriage quite well through either bad behaviour or bad communication, but let's not forget about the destructive effect of bad myths. Two such myths are especially deeply embedded in our culture. *"They lived happily ever after"* is one of them. They didn't live happily ever after, of course. They had rows, and they handled them well or badly as the rest of us do. They worked out ways of staying married in spite of their differences, or they couldn't handle their differences and got divorced, just like the rest of us do. But the myth of eternal happiness has buried itself in our thoughts and dreams so deeply that we assume somebody else can make us happy – until they don't.

The myth makes us dependent on the attitude and performance of the other person. In real life, happiness can be sustained only through our own attitude, not somebody else's performance. Sooner or later everybody lets us down, and we don't know how to handle it. They only lived happily ever after because they put the effort in to make it happen. More likely, they hung out for a few years, split up and continued on their disappointing, self-repeating cycle of failed relationships. The seemingly compelling myth encouraging us to *"follow your heart"* has much the same effect. Compelling it may be. But it's also entirely selfish. Follow your heart now and you'll surely follow your heart later when the other person fails to satisfy.

So now you know. You can destroy and undermine your own marriage very effectively with any one or more of the above techniques. Or you can make your marriage last by nipping any of these in the bud as you spot them popping out. It's entirely your choice!

Chapter 4 **Good habits**

In this chapter

- How a change in attitude can also change our feelings
- How to communicate over difficult issues
- How to resolve inevitable differences

Taking off the old *AND* putting on the new

Now that I've shown how our automatic negative patterns of behaviour, communication and belief can eat away at a relationship, I'm going to show you some ways of getting rid of these destructive patterns. We need to get rid of the old bad habits *and* learn new good habits. This can be extremely difficult, because old habits die hard. They become automatic precisely because they are so well ingrained and are therefore difficult to undo.

Awareness of bad habits is the first half of the battle. It is really important that support couples can identify and gently point out these destructive patterns. For example, if I know I tend to put Kate down when we argue, there's a chance I could choose not to do it any more. Of course, the reality is that this is difficult. When my emotions are running high or I forget what I've learned, back come the old habits.

Knowledge of good habits is the second half of the battle.

Good habits are primarily practical skills that you and I can use to start edging out our ingrained destructive behaviours.

I remember a few years ago having a coffee with some older friends of ours, Arthur and Jenny, whom we think of as our informal mentors. Kate and I were commiserating about how, although our own marriage kept getting better, we just couldn't seem to kick the same old bad habits that kept pulling us down when we least expected it. They were our *"crevasse"* moments. One moment, all is well. The next we have disappeared into a crevasse. We always knew it was a crevasse and not the end of our marriage. We now knew how to get out of the crevasse. But it always took time and pain until one of us swallowed our pride enough to take the first positive step to improve things.

I remember being quite dumbstruck when Arthur told us that *"after 35 years together, our marriage is almost effortless now"*. I had thought that effort was exactly what it took to build a great marriage. So I asked him to elaborate. He talked about all the regular little habits he and Jenny had built up over the years – ways of connecting with each other. By effortless, he meant that their good habits had become automatic. There was much less opportunity for the old habits to drag their marriage down. Their marriage had indeed taken effort. But all that effort was paying off.

Let's look now at how couples can put new constructive habits in place to replace the old destructive habits. Anyone can learn great marriage. Here is the seemingly unromantic guide to practical skills that work. These are good habits that any couple – yourselves included – can learn. Like any new skill, they won't seem natural at first. But just like learning to ride a bicycle, they become more natural with practice, and eventually effortless. I hope and expect that our marriage will be effortless one day.

A positive attitude

You'll have heard countless people explaining on TV, in magazines or in newspapers how their previous relationships failed because they weren't *"soulmates"* or it *"just wasn't meant to be"*. The implication is that if only they'd married the *"perfect person"*, things would have worked out. Recognise the myth?

This puts tremendous pressure on that other person to have the right characteristics, to perform in the right way and to meet their needs and expectations. It shifts the responsibility away from me to you. It's easier to blame you or the relationship than take responsibility for me.

The reality is that *my* relationship thrives or fails depending in large part on *my* attitude. By attitude, I mean what I think about somebody. How much I value them. The decisions and choices I make about that person. If I think somebody is important, I will probably be pleased to be around that person and will behave well. *"Where your treasure is, there shall your heart lie also"* has been a key principle for me in my marriage. What I value with my head, my heart will feel good about. Romance lasts when it starts in the head.

Does this sound unromantic? My wife, Kate, used to think so but she has reluctantly accepted that it is true. Let me give you an example of how attitude change can make a gigantic difference to how you feel about somebody.

Some years ago, I went to the theatre for an evening of entertainment with Dudley Moore. Worldwide, Dudley Moore was probably best known for his films *10* and *Arthur*. In the UK, most people knew him for his long-standing comic partnership with Peter Cook. Less well-known was that he was also an exceptionally gifted jazz pianist, one of the finest my country has produced. I was hugely looking forward to an evening out to hear him do both comedy and jazz live.

Unfortunately the evening fell some way short of my expectations. He was moderately amusing but not exceptionally so. His piano pastiches were still wonderful but far from his best. After the interval, he came out with a long iced drink in his hand and was slurring his words. The friend I had gone with was another big Dudley Moore fan, like me. After the show my friend was furious. How dare he make hundreds of loyal fans pay decent money for an evening out and then ruin it by getting tipsy? I was not as angry, but I remember leaving feeling distinctly unimpressed, disillusioned and sad that a talented man should let himself down so much.

Now cut forward a few years and I'm sitting down one evening watching TV at home. The programme is about Dudley Moore, who I am shocked to discover is dying of motor neurone disease. His brain is no longer functioning fully and he has months to live. He slurs his words so badly that you can hardly hear what he says. He can just about make himself understood well enough to tell us the very worst thing about his fatal disease. It is that he can sit in front of a piano and imagine the pieces he wants to play. But his fingers simply won't do what he tells them. It is heart-rending stuff and I am deeply shocked to see him like this.

I am suddenly taken back to that evening in the theatre several years earlier when he was slurring his words and clearly performing well below his best. A further shock is to realise that while we had automatically assumed he was drunk, in fact it was because his brain was being eaten away. I felt so ashamed of myself for the wrong assumption I had made. I also felt huge admiration for this man's courage in performing – one of the last times he did – in front of people, knowing that his talents were wasting away. Of course I felt compassion for his appalling illness and his frustration at no longer being able to play the piano.

The point of this story is in how what I knew in my head changed my feelings quite dramatically. What I thought I knew when I went to the theatre affected my attitude. My attitude affected my behaviour and my feelings. Then I felt anger, disillusionment and sadness. What I know now has completely changed the way I see things. Now I feel shame, admiration and compassion. The situation itself has not changed. But what I know now has affected my attitude and produced a completely different set of feelings. The diagrams illustrate how this works.

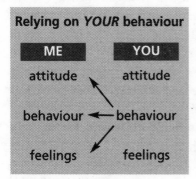

Figure 4.1 Behaviour

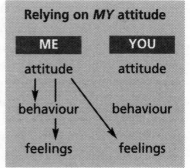

Figure 4.2 Attitude

The links between attitude, behaviour and feelings work both ways for me and for you. My attitude can influence my behaviour and feelings just as my feelings can influence my behaviour and my attitude. Which of these I rely on most is the critical factor.

I have a fundamental choice in my relationships. Either I can choose to rely more on my heart, which depends more on the other person's attitude, feelings and behaviour, or I can choose to rely more on my head, which will then determine my attitude, feelings and behaviour. Relying on my feelings in the theatre led me to a completely wrong conclusion about Dudley Moore. Relying on knowledge about the situation turned that conclusion on its head.

Yes, the system still works both ways. When my feelings are raw, it can be difficult to choose to love with my head. But having made that choice in advance gives me a better chance of surviving those raw feelings and not behaving badly for too long.

I decided long ago that my marriage is important and valuable. Because I try to keep that idea uppermost when things are going downhill, I can better withstand short-term negative feelings and our crevasses. It doesn't always work out. My feelings still lead me astray and old bad habits set in. In particular I opt out and think the worst. But when those feelings subside, I remember to behave better because I have decided to love Kate no matter what. The result is that our marriage is more stable in the long run and I feel more loving towards Kate more of the time.

"Where your treasure lies, your heart will lie also." When you choose to value something with your head – when you decide it is important – then the good feelings will follow.

A positive response to repair attempts

Ten years ago from the time of writing, my marriage to Kate nearly ended. At the heart of the problem was our lack of intimacy. In large part this was due to my inability to understand about relationships. Since my parents divorced when I was three, I had seen little of what an intact marriage looks like up close. I had seen commitment via my grandparents, but not the inner workings of a marriage. I had ideas about what marriage should be like, but no way of knowing whether my ideas were any good. I had also dealt with my childhood experiences by becoming very closed emotionally. Maybe lots of English men are closed. I was their team captain!

The result of all this was that, when I did get married, I rarely took issues of intimacy into account. Sure, I had a good career, so we did lots of interesting things together. Sure, we had a great social life. But over time, we ceased being friends and became more like flatmates. No wonder that Kate would become frustrated that I rarely took her feelings into account. I hadn't a clue what that meant anyway. In her anger, she would escalate to make her point – like the "Monty Python" Englishman who simply shouts more loudly at the foreigner who doesn't speak English. I was the foreigner who didn't understand the language of relationships. So Kate's actions merely confused me and I would withdraw to stay out of range. I'm guessing that we probably both put each other down because we couldn't understand each other and we assumed the worst.

If you had perhaps been thinking that I as the author of this book am an insufferable smart alec with a perfect marriage, think again! Until our turning point a few years ago, we had had eight years of marriage to develop and perfect the whole hatful of bad habits – scoring points, thinking the worst, opting out and putting down. Yes, we have found ways of keeping these at bay. But, believe me, they are still around one way and another. Bad habits die hard.

Choosing to value each other has undoubtedly made a big difference for us. I said earlier that bad habits mostly reflect a bad attitude. Changing my attitude has often allowed both of us to nip arguments in the bud. At the very least, it allows us to make up quickly after a row. Usually that means sticking a tongue out at each other. The US marriage expert John Gottman calls this a *"repair attempt"*.

Successful repair attempts are very good news for a marriage. An injection of very personal humour takes the situation away from conflict and bad attitude towards silliness, intimacy and fun. Couples who are good at repair attempts can even override the effects of too many STOP signs. So this is a good trick to perfect. Of course, failed repair attempts are bad news. A stuck-out tongue or cheesy look at the wrong moment can make a bad situation worse. I know personally how much of a kick in the guts it feels to have a repair attempt rebutted. So you need to pick your moment for these. Fortunately for us, when one of us sticks a tongue out, the other usually responds very quickly, we collapse in laughter and the row is over.

A positive communication skill

However...we also needed to learn how to communicate constructively, so that we could avoid getting into those bad habits in the first place. Over the years, Kate and I have learned a number of different positive communication skills. All these skills seem terribly unnatural. That may not be a bad thing. After all, STOP signs are natural, and they're not good. Kate and I have undoubtedly made huge breakthroughs using communication skills for the first time. But weeks or months later, we've forgotten them and revert to our old arguments. We lack the discipline to keep using new skills.

Many times I've seen this skill taught on its own as a healthy communication skill. Frankly, I think it comes across as namby-pamby and stupid because it lacks context. Real people don't use artificial communication skills. Research supports this. As Kate used to say to me a few years ago when I sat down and tried to use some newly-learned counselling skills, *"Don't you be a counsellor with me!"*

The key to this particular communication skill is to know that it's not for everyday life. It's there for special occasions when we need to talk safely about difficult issues without heading off into our old familiar destructive patterns. Positive communication is primarily a way of reducing negative behaviour.

So always remember it is the destructive behaviours we have to reduce or prevent. For Kate and me, it is still not normal. We'll use the skill *only* when we know we need to talk about something that normally causes us to argue. *"I don't want you to argue with me about this,"* Kate will say. *"I just need you to hear me out."* It's a positive communication skill because it prevents us from hurting each other.

So let's look again at the communication diagram (Figure 4.3). When I say something to you, I send a message giving you some information. I want to know that you have heard what I said and understood it. But how can I be really sure?

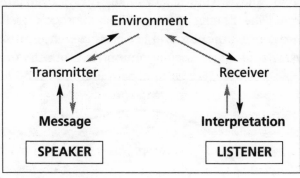

Figure 4.3 Two-way communication

You could reply in a number of ways that aren't quite adequate:

- You could nod your head. But that simply tells me your head is working
- You could say *"Yes, I understand."* But since I don't know how you think, I still couldn't be really certain you did understand

- You could repeat back to me what I said, word for word. That would certainly tell me you had heard what I said. But it wouldn't tell me that you had thought about it and understood.

Or you could do this:

- You could paraphrase back to me what I have said, using your own words. This tells me you have heard what I said because you have got the gist of it. But it also tells me you have understood because you have interpreted it in your own words.

Figure 4.4 shows what it looks like. The speaker passes the message. The listener interprets the message. The listener then replies by paraphrasing the message. The speaker then knows whether the message is interpreted correctly or not.

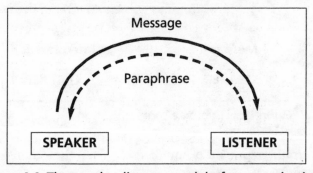

Figure 4.4 The speaker-listener model of communication

Does this sound unnatural and faintly ridiculous? Yes, of course it does. Its primary purpose is not to get you communicating better. It's to stop you communicating *badly*.

I give you two guarantees in teaching you this skill. First, as long as you use it correctly, it will enable you to discuss safely any difficult issue that would normally send you into a tizzy. Second, you and I will never use it for real unless we practise it. That's why, on our training courses for couples, we always set aside time for practice.

Paraphrase process

Paraphrasing is a simplified version of an active listening skill called "Speaker/Listener", taught on the well-researched PREP course. Paraphrasing works only when we have an issue to discuss that is likely to end in tears. We take it in turns to speak and listen because we are a team. Each of us has something to say. I need to get into your shoes and you need to get into mine.

When I say my bit, I need to concentrate on short bursts and to use *"I…"* language. That usually means starting sentences with the words *"I…"*, *"I think…"*, *"I feel…"* or *"It seems to me that…"* It also means avoiding starting sentences with the word *"You…"* It's tempting to keep on talking because I've got a lot to get off my chest. But short bursts mean you won't forget what I said first.

When you listen to me, you must just listen. Try not to think what you're going to say next. Try not to defend yourself or explain. Just tell me what I said in your own words. That usually means starting sentences with the words *"What you're saying is…"* or something similar. It also means avoiding starting sentences with the words *"But…"*, *"Because…"* or *"Why…"* These words all suggest you're not listening.

Example of a typical argument without paraphrase

Here's an example of an argument that develops because of poor communication:

What we actually say to each other	How we are communicating
Me: *"How come there was no food when I got home last night?"*	Me: Thinking the worst "You didn't cook" = "You don't care"
You: *"You were late again. I got fed up with waiting."*	You: "You…" = defensive "…again" = scoring points
Me: *"Yes, but you knew I was going to be late."*	Me: "But…" = not listening
You: *"Come on. It's hardly the first time. You were late on Tuesday. You were late last week."*	You: Almost attempts a repair but then expands the issue = scoring points
Me: *"You're not exactly the world's best timekeeper."*	Me: Fails to respond to repair attempt. Put-down and further scoring points
You: *"Huh? Look. You haven't even asked me how my day was."*	You: "Huh" = contempt "You…" = scoring points
Me: *"I give up…"*	Me: Opting out

Example of argument with paraphrase

We decide we want to talk about it later using paraphrase:

What we actually say to each other	How we are communicating
Me: *"I was really hungry when I got back. I thought you were going to leave me some food."*	Me: Good use of "I…" and "My" thoughts rather than making assumption about "You"
You: *"You were surprised I hadn't cooked for you."*	You: Good straightforward paraphrase. No defensive explanation attempted
Me: *"Yes. I was really tired. I'd had a bad day and I was really looking forward to having dinner with you."*	Me: Feeling understood encourages further explanation. Expresses "my" feelings and "my" disappointment
You: *"You thought a cosy chat with me would be a good end to a bad day."*	You: Excellent paraphrase although not 100% right
Me: *"Not quite. It didn't need to be cosy, just a relaxed dinner together."*	Me: Clarifies that the event is more important than the setting
You: *"So you didn't want the full roaring fire and rug treatment, just the kitchen table."*	You: Gets it right this time
Me: *"Yes. Exactly."*	Me: Confirms

We then exchange roles:

What we actually say to each other	How we are communicating
You: *"OK. I had dinner for you waiting two hours before you got back. What was I to do?"*	You: Although clearly cross, "I" words keep it personalised
Me: *"You did cook me dinner, just long before I actually returned."*	Me: Paraphrases well. Doesn't defend
You: *"Yes. And I just got really cross waiting for you. Humf."*	You: Signs of a repair attempt
Me: *"You were miffed with me."*	Me: Paraphrases well. Responds positively to repair attempt
You: *"Yes. I wanted a quiet dinner too and I didn't know you were going to be so late."*	You: Keeps it personalised and adds further explanation

At this point, hopefully I apologise and we melt into each other's arms. Of course a positive attitude from me – in the shape of a simple apology and a little humility – would undoubtedly have done much to diffuse the argument in the first place. But the addition of good communication skills has brought us together and added a moment of real intimacy.

Positive problem-solving

I said earlier that the point of paraphrasing is to encourage more positive communication on difficult subjects. There will be some occasions, such as in the example above, when the differences between the man and the woman are about feelings, expectations and perceptions. Paraphrasing works well on these and can lead to a complete resolution. Instead of *"You made me cross"* leading to *"Well, don't blame me"*, you get *"I'm cross"* leading to *"I'm sorry."* Paraphrasing makes it harder to be aggressive or defensive to each other and easier for both to feel understood.

But there are guaranteed to be plenty of occasions when husbands and wives simply can't agree or work things out. They may have very different attitudes indeed to any number of subjects – children, money, sex, in-laws, work, hobbies, time, romance, etc. Communication is a skill for discussing our differences. *"I think this. You think that. Great. Now we need to sort it out."* Problem-solving is a skill for resolving these differences.

There are all sorts of complicated problem-solving models around. This simple problem-solving model is one of the neatest and most powerful I've seen. I'm a fan because it's revolutionised an area of my own marriage that had plagued Kate and me for years. Let me explain the basic idea and then I'll show you our example.

The model starts off with a good and thorough discussion. We need to understand each other's position. The better we understand each other, the more likely we are to find a long-lasting solution that works for both of us. Shallow discussions lead to shallow solutions. After that we need pen and paper to write down our ideas and our solution. If we don't write it down, it'll get forgotten.

There are four steps:

1. We write the problem down: *"You think this, I think that, we need to sort it out."*
2. We brainstorm all ideas and write them down, however silly or implausible – without comment, eye-rolling or tongue-clicking.
3. We agree on what we can and write that down.
4. We book a follow-up date in the diary to see if our solution has worked.

Our real life example of problem-solving

Kate and I needed to deal with a problem that had plagued our marriage for fifteen years. We started with a long discussion. Kate thrives on having people around and offering hospitality. I am utterly unpredictable at social events – sometimes charming; sometimes sharp, dismissive and rude. This sends Kate into a panic. When other people were around us at home, our relationship became somewhat strained...

1. We wrote down the problem like this: *"What pushes Harry's buttons? What causes panic in Kate? How do we reduce these?"*

2. Then we started brainstorming, writing it all down as we thought of ideas.

    I started with a brilliant idea: *"Kate checks with Harry before agreeing any social events."* Kate couldn't see how this would change things when people were actually there. She suggested that *"Harry is open and welcoming to anybody who comes into the house"*. She then thought a post-mortem worthwhile: *"Harry agrees to discuss problems with Kate afterwards."*

    Meanwhile, I was beginning to feel the pressure on me. So I made the rather fatuous suggestion that *"We have no social events unless Harry agrees"*, to which Kate's obvious retort was *"We have an open door and anyone comes in"*. I wasn't being too serious when I lowered the tone by suggesting *"Harry behaves as he wishes and Kate lets him"*. Kate put me back in my box by demanding that *"Harry stays charming all the time"*.

Common sense returned and Kate volunteered: *"Harry explains his discomfort at the time and asks for allowance."* This was very helpful to me. I tried to think of genuine solutions such as *"No social events planned after a weekly deadline"*. I also didn't want to change Kate. I had married her for the way she is, bubbly and spontaneous. It would be a crime to stifle that deliberately, so I said: *"Harry allows Kate to be spontaneous."* That opened the door to the solution, which Kate proffered: *"Kate asks Harry about social events rather than tells him."* In fact this was much the same as I had said earlier. The difference was that it came from Kate.

3. We both then agreed on what we could. It was fairly easy to agree that *"SPONTANEITY is the key issue for Kate"* and *"PARTICIPATION in the process is the hidden issue for Harry"*. This was interesting because it helped Kate realise that people were not the problem. She had always suspected that my unpredictability was because I saw people as obstructions to our time or my work. Working from home had presented us with quite a few difficulties. We were able to agree, as a bonus, that Kate could expect nothing from me during work hours unless previously arranged.

We then agreed that Kate could suggest social plans as questions not statements. Although Kate agreed to this, she said she found it difficult to say things in the right way. We were now treating each other very gently and were very quick to be constructive. It was therefore easy to agree that the way Kate speaks to me is important but that Kate finds word order very hard. I agreed to be gracious if Kate got that wrong. We returned to the subject by agreeing that I could check what was expected of me at a social event. We also agreed that having people in the house was of great benefit to us, even essential. What a contrast to my silly idea during the brainstorm! Kate then told me that working together with me was a bonus.

4. We wrote down our solution: *"Kate will check with Harry before confirming – the key issue here is Harry's PARTICIPA-TION. Where Kate can't check back, Harry will ask what is required and be gracious – the key issue here is Kate's SPON-TANEITY."* We agreed to follow up at our next *"date night"*, our weekly evening we reserved for us no matter what.

It's been a fantastic solution that has transformed our social life. Admittedly, we had a hiccup about 18 months later and cracks appeared in our solution. But we talked it over and reviewed this same solution – which was easy, as we'd written it all down.

So if Kate invites you to our house today, expect to hear her confirm *"I just need to check with Harry."* When you get here, you will find me all sweetness and light!

When you can't find a solution

There will be times when two people have positions that are intractable and irreconcilable. That doesn't mean it's time to rush off to the divorce courts. The justification of divorce due to "irreconcilable differences" sounds like a pretty pathetic excuse to many children of divorce – if anyone bothered to ask the kids.

The truth is that even the most successful couples have irreconcilable differences. Professor John Gottman claims that 60% of all differences between husband and wife are never reconciled. Do they divorce? No. They make their marriage work in spite of their differences.

Kate and I have all sorts of differences, especially regarding children and money. Kate went to a comprehensive school that taught her loads about relationships and nothing about education. I went to a top private school where I learned loads about education and nothing about relationships. Our reactions are fairly predictable. Kate's highest priority for our children is a good education. My highest priority for them is that they learn how to relate well. We are poles apart. In practice, we try to ensure that our kids get a bit of both. But it's still a thorny issue whenever it comes up. We just don't let it trash our marriage. After all, the best gift we can give the kids is our marriage. Likewise, we have hugely different attitudes to money. I see money as a commodity to be used as necessary. Kate sees money as a store of value to be built up over time. Money is definitely a thorny issue for us. But again we don't let it trash our marriage.

There will definitely be times when a problem appears to have no solution. We can discuss it at length. We can use the problem-solving method. The original problem starts with *"I want kids now. You want to wait five years"*. We brainstorm all sorts of ideas but then we simply can't agree. So what happens next? The way ahead is to accept that we are different and that we have different positions. We need to ask ourselves a new question: *"How are we going to stop this problem from trashing our marriage?"*

When we choose to love each other with a positive attitude in spite of our differences, when we choose to communicate positively to prevent us from hurting each other, then we can use the problem-solving method to find a way to accommodate our inevitable irreconcilable differences.

Summary

Old habits die hard. But the good news is that new habits can be learned. As support couples, we need to raise awareness of the bad habits and reinforce the good ones. In this chapter, we've looked at good habits that are designed to reduce the bad ones. Good habits don't seem natural and they aren't. So they need practice until they do become natural and we can use them when we need them.

The first good habit is a positive change in attitude. Destructive behaviours in a relationship come from a bad attitude – whether defending myself or attacking you or both. When I see you as different and scary or threatening, I will behave badly and I will feel negative towards you. When I see you as valuable and worth cherishing, I will value you and cherish you with my behaviour. My feelings towards you will be positive.

I may not have a choice about my feelings – they are spontaneous. If I rely on what I feel, I will be blown along by what you do, how you behave and how that makes me feel. But I do have a choice about my attitude. Loving you means choosing to see you as valuable, no matter what you do. When I do that, my behaviour and heart will follow. The whole process of love starts in my head. Although it doesn't stop us having rows and niggles, at the very least it allows us to respond quickly when one of us reaches out and makes an attempt to repair things.

The second good habit is to learn a safe way to discuss difficult issues. Active listening skills are far from natural. Kate and I hardly ever use them. Yet we know how to paraphrase when we need to. Paraphrasing is highly effective at reducing all the STOP signs that usually reflect a bad attitude. The secret is to try to learn what it is like to be the other person. Repeating back word for word shows that the message has been heard. Paraphrasing shows that the message has been both heard *and* understood. We all feel a whole lot more open to one another when we feel understood.

The third good habit is knowing how to resolve differences. The key to this is a thorough discussion beforehand. Shallow discussions produce shallow solutions. After discussing our differences, we write down the problem, brainstorm any possible ideas without comment, agree on what we can, and book a time to follow up whether our solution has worked. When we can't agree on a solution, we have a new problem – how to prevent the problem from wrecking our marriage.

Chapter 5   **Party tricks**

In this chapter

- How to discover the best way to love others
- How to meet each other's needs
- How to break a repeating pattern or communication deadlock

Party tricks to melt the ice and make a couple happy

"When I fall in love, it will be forever", sang Nat King Cole, I seem to recall. And pretty much all of us have this happy dream in our minds when we do fall in love. We want this great gushing feeling that overwhelms us now to last for ever. The slap in the face comes months or years later as it dawns on us that happy feelings don't last for ever. They come and go. How many Hollywood film stars do we see canoodling lovingly for the paparazzi cameras after their wedding? Around three years later, just as the drug rush in their heads runs out, we see the very same couple peering lovingly into the cameras once again. Only this time it's not with each other. They express their regrets at the inevitable passing of the marriage and say how happy they are with their new partners. The destructive cycle is ready to repeat itself once more. If only they'd known that great marriage can be learned.

In the previous two chapters we've looked at bad habits that slowly eat away at a marriage and at good habits that kick the bad ones into touch. The key here is stability. Bad habits and good habits are all about whether you're going to make it. But just as long-lasting marriages may not be happy, happy marriages may not be long-lasting. We need both stability AND happiness.

As support couples, we're interested in pointing out patterns. We now know how to spot the more natural bad habits – bad behaviours, bad communication and bad beliefs. We know how to encourage and affirm the less natural good habits – positive attitude, a positive communication skill and a positive problem-solving skill. What we need now are some party tricks that help couples develop habits that build happiness.

I call the ideas in this chapter *"party tricks"* because they're amusing and insightful and have immediate impact. But, just as with happiness, their effect won't necessarily last. They are all ways of boosting our feelings for each other by helping us understand each other better. They raise our awareness. The more we know, the more we are likely to behave with consideration.

Researchers who conduct surveys of couples tell us that communication and happiness are virtually indistinguishable from one another. The formula is simple and direct. Whereas communication is only one of many factors that influence stability, communication is pretty much the only factor that influences happiness. Good communication equals happy couples. Poor communication equals unhappy couples. And, as with good and bad habits, we do both at different times depending on what we decide, what's going on and how we feel.

So for support couples, here are some party tricks that will often have immediate impact on a couple. When people hear these ideas for the first time, they often say they wish they'd known this sort of stuff before. *"It's such common sense. Perhaps I wouldn't have got divorced."* It can begin to sound like a miracle cure. Nothing wrong with a miracle cure as long as you know its limitations. On its own, it won't keep the all-important bad habits at bay for very long. Another way is to think of these tricks as being like a bar of chocolate or a cup of coffee. It feels great while you're eating or drinking it. But the effects are quickly forgotten.

So let's say you are mentoring a couple. You've already spent an evening or two with them, so you've got to know each other a bit. At least you've broken the ice. But tonight your couple just can't seem to see eye to eye. They seem to be communicating at cross-purposes. You suspect they probably had a row before they arrived. Their body language seems closed. Their comments are abrupt. They're not putting their hearts into it. They're not even willing to use their heads and decide to love one another. They hate paraphrasing and won't use it. They're in a grump. What you need are some party tricks!

Party trick 1: Love languages

This is my particular favourite. Kate and I have found it very helpful as a married couple and as parents. If you want a lot more, then read the book *The Five Love Languages* by Gary Chapman. If you want a little more, then read the chapter in Nicky and Sila Lee's excellent *The Marriage Book*, which also covers the subject really well.

The principle of love languages is simple. There are supposedly five main ways in which love can be given and received – through WORDS, ACTIONS, TOUCH, GIFTS and TIME. Everybody is different. Most people find that one or more of these five ways is natural to them. Most people also tend to give out love to others in the way they wish to be loved themselves. If TOUCH is the most important aspect of love for a husband, he may show his love for his wife by hugging her often. Yet if TIME is the most important aspect of love to the wife, these hugs may become an irritant because her husband does not spend the time with her that she needs to feel loved. Once a husband and wife have discussed and identified their love languages, it can help to reduce the wrong assumptions they make. They can not only reduce such misunderstandings but also increase their ways of showing love that will be received as such.

Kate and I are fairly stereotypical as a husband and wife. I'm a natural introvert. I tend to relax by hanging out on my own and not with other people. I show love to others by doing things for them or with them. I empty bins and make beds and collect the kids from school and change nappies. But I also show love by giving Kate hugs. So my love languages are ACTIONS and TOUCH. I receive love most powerfully from Kate when she does something *for* me – such as cooking or bathing the kids – or does something *with* me – such as when we do mentoring together. I also receive love when she touches me or says yes in the evening.

Kate, however, is a natural extrovert. She tends to relax by hanging out with people rather than on her own. She shows love to others by spending time with them, chatting with them and doing things together. Her love languages are WORDS and TIME. Kate receives love most powerfully from me when I hang out with her and chat, such as by lying on our bed in the evening or by having dinner together. She also receives love when I do something with her.

Unfortunately, knowing all this is both awful and wonderful. It's awful because we are still who we are. Our natural states are still very different. Because Kate doesn't naturally think about ACTIONS or TOUCH, I can end up feeling disconnected from her. Because I don't naturally think about WORDS and TIME, Kate can end up feeling disconnected from me. Our communication suffers and we spark off each other more easily. We then both revert to our natural bad habits of escalation and withdrawal. Our happiness will suddenly plummet, triggered by the smallest of reasons. When our natural states take over and we fall into a hole, it can be hard to decide to love the way we each receive love – even though we know perfectly well how to love each other in each other's respective love language. Kate doesn't naturally want to do things for me or touch me. I don't naturally want to hang out and chat with her.

But it's wonderful because, at some point, one of us will decide to be the grown up and do something out of character. Kate will put her hand on my shoulder. As long as she doesn't grimace while she does it, I feel supported and loved. My attitude immediately improves; I behave more positively and our marriage starts spiralling back upwards instead of down. Or I will decide to hang out with Kate in the evening. We talk about how the kids are getting on, some admin. problems that have been preying on her mind, my work, or anything. Kate feels supported and loved. Her attitude becomes softer towards me and our marriage spirals back upwards again instead of down.

Kate and I have also used the love-language idea with our kids. We have six children and that's quite enough, we hope. Recently, we were going through one of those periodic parenting dramas when we didn't seem to be connecting with our two eldest children. On a car journey, we decided to tell them about the idea of love languages. For one of them, it was easy to identify TIME and ACTIONS as her love languages. Normally, this worked well for both Kate and me. She would hang out with Kate and they would do something like cooking together. She would encourage me to help her make things. The lack of connection was because Kate and I had a particular time pressure at that moment. We talked it through and fairly quickly found ways to rectify it.

With the other child, identifying her love language was much less obvious and took quite a bit of probing. We started by asking her what she thought. She said she wanted TIME. Yet the evidence was that she rarely volunteered to spend time with us. Whenever we encouraged her to hang out with us, she would seem to disappear and prefer playing with her siblings or friends – anyone but us. Eventually we reversed the question and asked her when she had felt loved by us. Playing games together, she said. Arranging games with one child when you have six is not obviously easy – nor is it either of our love languages, so we don't do it naturally. Kate wants to chat. I want to do things for others, more than play with them.

So it turned out that ACTIONS was her love language. However, she was waiting for us to arrange games with her, which we didn't because it didn't occur to either of us. Having explained this, we asked what she could do to help herself. Her own solution came from writing down her special weekly time with us on our kitchen calendar. That way, she increased her chances of getting loved the way she wanted and we could then give her that love.

As a support couple, you can talk about the idea of love languages very easily. You don't need to be an expert in order to understand the idea or help a couple to apply it themselves. But it's a very useful trick for breaking the ice when a couple either won't talk or seem to misunderstand each other. It helps a couple identify and acknowledge each other's difference.

All you need to do is explain that we all tend to give love in the same way we best receive it. There are five of these love languages – WORDS, ACTIONS, TOUCH, GIFTS and TIME. Most people find one or two of these love languages especially important. You then ask them to try to work out which languages go with which person. They could write it down and try to guess the other's love language. Or you can just get them to discuss it. Finally, you can encourage them to work out specific ways of doing things for each other using their language. How can they make that a habit rather than just a nice thing to do tomorrow? It'll work like magic.

Party trick 2: Emotional needs

From much the same school of understanding differences comes the idea of *"emotional needs"*. This is also an idea that has immediate impact and appeal. *"A-ha"*, she says, *"at last he understands me!"*

My personal preference is for love languages because they are a bit easier to remember and seem to focus more on the other person. But many others think emotional needs are the business. In reality, I'm not sure it matters much. They do much the same job.

The idea of emotional needs probably originates from a psychologist called Abraham Maslow back in the 1950s. He described a "hierarchy of needs" leading to what he called "self-actualisation". Much of the counselling industry has this idea at its core.

At the bottom of the pile is our need to survive. We need food, water and shelter. Everything else is secondary. At the top of the pile is our need for aesthetics. Having met all other needs, we may find we need particular symmetry and order and beauty around us. In between are various layers that reflect the needs of our heart and head.

Emotional needs are the behaviours we most crave from others. Figure 5.1 shows a typical list.

I need:	
• ACCEPTANCE	– give me confidence that I'm OK
• AFFECTION	– reassure me with words or touches
• APPRECIATION	– say nice things about what I do
• APPROVAL	– say nice things about who I am
• ATTENTION	– acknowledge that what I do is OK
• COMFORT	– be alongside me
• ENCOURAGEMENT	– give me confidence to keep going
• RESPECT	– say nice things about where I have got to
• SECURITY	– give me confidence that you will stay with me
• SUPPORT	– help me do things

Figure 5.1 Emotional needs

As with love languages, most of us automatically assume you and I have the same needs. Unlike with food or décor or Christmas presents, where I realise we have different tastes, it just doesn't occur to me that we have different needs. Realising we are different is the first part of the battle. If I know what Kate's needs are and Kate knows what my needs are, we can tailor our behaviour to meet each other's needs.

Strong or seemingly inappropriate emotions are often a sign of unmet needs. We react badly when we feel hurt, angry, guilty, anxious or stressed. When we are hurt, we need comfort. When we are angry, we need to forgive. When we feel guilty, we need to say sorry. When we feel anxious, we need someone to share it with. When we are stressed, we need somebody to help us.

Because it's hard to know other people's needs, we have to tell one another. This is an ideal task for support couples. Get your couple to face away from each other and write down their top three needs and their spouse's top three needs from the list above. Then get them to face each other and see how many they got right. Very few couples can guess accurately which are the most important two or three needs of their spouse. Ask them to tell each other what they can do specifically to meet these specific needs. More magic!

Here are some examples:

* Tom says he needs COMFORT. His wife suggests that she can give him more hugs. He explains that hugs are fine but all he really needs is for her to sit next to him on the sofa occasionally in the evenings. Being next to him for a period of time is the crucial ingredient.

* Mary says she needs SECURITY. Her husband says he changed all the locks last week. She appreciates that but explains that actually she wants him to complete a will. Knowing that the future is planned is more important than her physical security.

* Brian says he needs ATTENTION. His wife tells him she loves him. He says he knows that and it's great. What he really needs is for her to ask him how his day has been when he comes home from work. He wants her to show interest in what he's doing.

* Sue says she needs APPRECIATION. Her husband suggests he will compliment her more often on how she looks. She says that would be nice. But she'd especially

like him to comment on home life – appreciating the food she has cooked or how tidy the house is.

Party trick 3: The dance

This is a good one. "The dance" is an idea suggested by another psychologist, Sherod Miller, who developed a programme called Relationship Education which has been popular in the US for decades. His approach works on the principle that communication, negotiation and conflict resolution involve much more than words. The way we communicate non-verbally, with our actions, is far more powerful. This is not a million miles away from what either PREP or Gottman also says. The biggest predictors of future trouble are found among the unhealthy automatic patterns of behaviour we get into whenever we argue.

Kate and I have used "the dance" successfully in a number of different circumstances, when we've been mentoring couples getting married or already-married couples who are going through a tough time. Firstly, the dance is a really good framework for identifying and understanding any repeating pattern of behaviour. It's different because it sticks to non-verbals rather than teaching skills. Secondly it's a really good framework for working out a more constructive way of dealing with these situations. It's especially helpful when only one person realises there's a problem and the other doesn't. As part of a support couple, this is a party trick I'd use when I see a fairly stubborn kind of deadlock.

Let me give you an example of when to use it. A couple tell you: *"We always seem to argue whenever the subject of X is raised."* You as support couples know that they must find a way of dealing with this. Otherwise the subject will trigger bad behaviours that will render that whole subject a no-go area. You've discussed the STOP signs. You know they keep cropping up. You've tried to get the couple to paraphrase to discuss the issue. But each time they seem unable to prevent their emotions from taking over. They interrupt each other or defend themselves. Nothing seems to work. This will. But be careful and gentle when you use it. It can be quite a powerful technique.

The dance is a game played on an imaginary draughts or chessboard covering the floor of a room. The two players, the couple, start the game near the middle of the board, facing each other with one empty square between them. The rules are simple. Players take it in turns to move. A move can consist of a single step to an adjacent square – whether forward, back, or to either side. A move can also consist of a turn on the same square – whether turning through 90 degrees or 180 degrees. A player can do only one of these moves during their turn. It's then the turn of the other player. Players have the option of staying still during their turn. The game ends when a pattern starts to repeat itself.

The idea now is to get the couple to work out their behaviour in terms of the dance. Let's start with a very simple example. Every time John and Jane talk about money, they have a row. Jane usually ends up getting cross and John usually ends up walking out of the room. It's an obvious repeating pattern. What does it look like in terms of the dance? John and Jane start the game one square apart, facing each other. Jane is usually the one to bring up the subject of money. So in the game she takes one step forward towards John. John sees this as confrontation. Jane is now right in front of him and he doesn't like it one bit. He feels threatened because he thinks Jane is checking up on him and doesn't trust him. He also knows that the last few times they've talked about money, they ended up arguing. So John's first move in the game is one step backwards. Although he wants to stay connected with Jane, he just doesn't want to have to deal with the issue. Jane, however, does want to deal with the issue. She sees John take a step back and she starts to feel frustrated that he won't talk about it. Her second move is to take a further step forward. She presses him. Don't run away. We need to work this out. But John feels more threatened. He can see trouble brewing and needs to avoid it. He takes a second step back. A basic pattern is starting to repeat itself already. In effect, Jane is escalating while John is withdrawing. A destructive unresolved argument with lots of bad feelings ensues. Jane feels frustrated, angry, disappointed and hurt perhaps. John feels threatened, protective and defensive.

So let's start the game again and see what happens when we change the dance. We want to help them find a way to break the destructive pattern. After Jane steps forward, instead of stepping back as he normally would, John actually has a number of choices. He could stay absolutely still. What does this mean in real life? John would be continuing to talk about the issue instead of seeking to avoid it. So he'd be saying something like, OK, let's talk. How would that feel for John? Very uncomfortable. It might even feel frightening because men don't trust themselves to behave calmly when faced with conflict in the home. He desperately doesn't want to hurt Jane but he fears he might do so if pushed too hard. So he's now standing there agreeing to face the issue but feeling very uncomfortable. The key now is Jane's next move. If she understands how difficult he is finding this, she might now take a step back in response to his discomfort. John could then be so relieved at the care she is showing that he might even take a step forward, thereby effectively now volunteering to talk about the issue. The pattern has been broken by John's decision to hold his ground and by Jane's decision to back off but stay engaged. That's one possible solution that could actually work for them. It's a fairly risky strategy because it needs John to stay in control of his fears long enough to let Jane take off the pressure.

All dances have a number of different solutions. Some will work better than others. In this case, although we've already found something that works, it's an uncomfortable solution. When Jane steps forward at the beginning, it may be that John still feels so threatened that he simply has to step back. As they talk through the dance, Jane now understands how threatened John feels. Instead of stepping forward for her second move, she might now stand still or even step back. What standing still might equate to in real life would be saying, I need to talk about this and I'm here when you're ready. John then feels less threatened and may even feel safe enough to step tentatively forward so that they are right next to each other. This new dance requires Jane's understanding and acceptance to change the pattern.

A third option might be to suggest that John try turning sideways when Jane steps forward. That way he isn't seen to be stepping backwards but nor would he have to face the perceived threat quite so directly. It might feel safer for him. However, Jane might then say this would drive her nuts. She would then manoeuvre sideways over the next few turns until she had got back in his face again and confronted him. This new dance clearly wouldn't work.

John and Jane might conclude that, next time the subject of money comes up, John should attempt to stay engaged by standing his ground. Jane will hopefully realise he is trying to respond so she will then back off. Should he start by taking his normal step back, Jane knows to stand her ground instead of stepping forward. She waits. Hopefully, John will then respond by stepping forward and engaging once again, rather than retreating.

As support couples, your role is simply to make suggestions that translate the dance into real life and vice versa. These are the kind of questions to ask: *"John, you'd normally step forward at this point. If you were to step sideways instead, what would that mean in real life?"* and then *"Jane, how would that feel to you, when you see John stepping sideways instead of forwards as you expected?"* Your aim is to get the couple to recognise a repeating pattern and work through various alternative moves that would break that pattern. How achievable are the new moves? What happens if one person regresses to the old pattern?

Kate and I like this idea. It combines what I've called bad habits – which are essentially repeating patterns anyway – with a problem-solving method. The great thing is that it requires a lot less verbal communication, since the non-verbals speak so powerfully for themselves. Just be tentative in what you suggest and what you see. The couple will do the work themselves. More magic.

Summary

In the two previous chapters, I've looked at the bad habits that eat away at a relationship over time and can lead to divorce, and I've looked at some good habits that reduce these bad ones. But now there is happiness to consider. This chapter shows a handful of ways to break communication roadblocks and make a marriage go with a swing. I call them party tricks because their effects are immediate but don't necessarily last. Try them on your friends!

The first of these is love languages. This is the idea that there are five main ways of communicating love – through WORDS, ACTIONS, TOUCH, GIFTS and TIME. Each of us tends to give out love in the way we want to receive it because we assume that everybody is the same. Figuring out your own and your spouse's love language can improve the odds that love will be received as intended. It has worked for us and we've even applied the idea to the children.

The second idea, emotional needs, works on similar principles. Each of us has different needs. If you identify the needs and meet them, you end up with a happier husband or wife. Personally, I prefer the idea of love languages because they come across as less self-centred and are easier to remember. But lots of people find the idea of emotional needs very helpful.

The third idea, the dance, is quite different. When couples row again and again over the same things, it may be that they are repeating a pattern of behaviour. One way of breaking such behaviour is to think of them as players on a draughts board. Each of them takes it in turns to move once or not at all. The key is to figure out what their behaviour looks like in terms of the game. Once you've done that, you can experiment with different moves to break the pattern. Then you have to ask what a move in the game would mean in real life. This is a powerful tool because it works on non-verbal communication.

Each of these party tricks can be really helpful in giving a couple a leg up or in dealing with communication roadblocks. Each of them usually has a fairly immediate impact. Just don't expect the effects to last. Finally, as always in mentoring, be sensitive to the situation when using these tricks.

Chapter 6   **Mentoring made easy**

In this chapter

- What an inventory is
- How inventories make mentoring easy
- What inventories can and cannot tell you

Further information on inventories

- FOCCUS – www.foccus.co.uk (UK) or www.foccusinc.com (US and elsewhere)
- PREPARE – www.prepare-enrich.co.uk (UK) or www.prepare-enrich.com (US and elsewhere)
  (*For full details see Appendix C.*)

Inventories – just like taking a couple around a supermarket...

Having taken you through the skills that will make you an excellent support couple, I'm now going to explain why mentoring is easy even without these skills.

All I want you to grasp is why strangely-named creatures called "inventories" have revolutionised marriage education. This introductory section tells you all you need to know, in the language of shopping. You could skip the rest of the chapter if you don't want to delve into the more technical aspects. Alternatively, if you can't stand shopping, skip this first section and read the rest of the chapter instead!

Mentoring with an inventory is a bit like taking a couple shopping. Before you go shopping, you start off in the kitchen looking around and writing down anything that comes to mind in any old order. You end up with a long list of items. When you get to the supermarket, you find that all the items you want are neatly arranged in aisles under various headings. Even though your shopping list is scrambled up, by the time you have been up and down every aisle, you will have bought everything you need because everything is so well organised and thorough – topic by topic, item by item. This includes all the items that hadn't even occurred to you back in the kitchen.

Marriage inventories are simply a list of statements about marriage, initially in any old order just like a real scrambled-up shopping list. Couples respond to these statements separately by saying *"I agree"* or *"I disagree"*. So it's as if each person has started off in their own separate kitchen and made two completely different shopping lists. Those answers then get combined and sorted into their relevant topics, just as each supermarket aisle is organised thoroughly into topics with lots of items. The organised list of responses is then returned to the support couple. That organised list is the equivalent of the supermarket.

Your job as the support couple is then to walk the couple up and down each aisle until you've covered everything. As you pass each item, you ask them to talk about it. From their combined shopping lists, they might have both agreed or both disagreed. Or they might have different opinions. Or they might have changed their minds. Either way, it's the fact that they think about each item and discuss it that counts.

You can share your own experience of each item if it seems relevant. That's about it!

What inventories do is make it easy and non-threatening for an ordinary married couple to mentor a couple as they work through their own specific issues. Note that the couple do the work, not you. They do the talking. You do the walking. It really is as easy as taking them out shopping. If you can keep that idea in your mind, you'll find mentoring a doddle. Here's why:

- Shopping isn't a test. You wouldn't say: *"You chose apples. He chose pears. Both of you are wrong!"*
- You don't need to be taught. You wouldn't say: *"Let me explain how beans are canned..."*
- You don't need to be counselled. You wouldn't say: *"How do you feel when he buys shampoo?"*
- You don't need to be an expert. You wouldn't say: *"87% of dogs choose Cat brand..."*
- All you do need to do is raise awareness of differences. In that case you might say: *"He likes Indian food. She likes Chinese food. Great. You're different! How about curry with spring rolls?"*

Finally, just as shopping lists don't determine whether a couple should go shopping together, neither do the inventories tell a couple whether they should get married or not. Couples have to decide that for themselves.

Inventories – the revolution in marriage education

You can either skip to the next chapter now or let me tell you a bit more about how inventories have revolutionised marriage education.

Around the world, a million couples a year use an inventory as a marriage preparation course. That includes around 20% of weddings in the US and 15% in Australia. Since the late 1990s, inventories have become increasingly easily available in the UK. As if with a wave of the magic wand, inventories have made mentoring easy and accessible to the least expert and most ordinary couple. That's because inventories ARE the expert.

Relationship inventories are a relatively new development of the personality inventories often used by businesses. The relationship inventory is a list of statements grouped into a range of different topics. The difference is that both the male and the female make separate responses to each statement on separate response sheets. The processed results show the combined level of agreement on each statement and topic. These "unscrambled" responses form the basis of further discussion by the couple.

Whereas individual inventories are almost always intended to provide analysis and interpretation, my own view is that relationship inventories should not. One inventory, called PREPARE, does. Another inventory, called FOCCUS, does not. What they all aim to do, however, is raise awareness and get couples talking. This is done with either a single facilitator or a support couple. The responses to each statement provide the framework for discussion. *"John agreed, Jane disagreed – talk to each other!"* Some facilitators don't even bother referring to the original responses. How the couple discuss the statement is the important thing.

The percentage level of agreement in each topic simply guides the facilitator as to whether a couple will have to work harder or less hard on their relationship overall or mostly on certain areas. As the couple discuss their responses to each statement and topic, they may open up areas of their relationship that had not previously been considered or discussed. They will then discover whether they agree or disagree on those areas, and may need to discuss them further. What the inventory DOES NOT say is whether a couple should get married or not. Nor can or should the facilitator or support couple say that.

Research on inventories

Pretty much anybody could put together a relationship inventory based on what they think is important. In the same way, anybody could put together a new marriage or relationship course. Use of that inventory or course might or might not then make a difference to a couple's future. It could be spot on and reflect processes and principles common to all couples or it might simply reflect the writer's prejudices and world view. Without objective research (*"Did you buy the right ingredients?"*), which is completely different from feedback and course evaluation (*"Did you enjoy shopping?"*), there's no way of knowing any of this for sure.

There are currently only two research-based couple inventories in the UK – FOCCUS and PREPARE/ENRICH. In the US, a third inventory is also available, called RELATE. Much excellent research has gone into putting these inventories together in the first place. But it's the research on how couples respond to the inventory now compared to how they actually behave later on that is most relevant for us as users.

Most of the dozen or so inventory studies involve the PREPARE/ENRICH group of five inventories (Fowers *et al.*, 1996). Where FOCCUS has been studied, methods and results look similar. In fact an independent study that compared the two found they were essentially similar (Williams & Jurich, 1995).

Research on inventories is very good. Inventories have tremendous strengths. But, as always with research, it's worth knowing the weaknesses as well. Below are the three major findings that I think are the most important from this research, along with the limitations that need highlighting.

Finding 1: Inventories can predict relationship success and failure accurately

When couples complete an inventory, their answers are combined and sorted into topics. Under each topic – such as children, or communication, or personality – there will be a score representing the percentage of statements with which the couple both agree. Those scores combine to form a profile. Several studies of PREPARE, ENRICH and FOCCUS inventories have found that those who end up happily married up to five years later had one type of profile, the unhappily married a second type, those who cancelled their weddings a third, and the separated/divorced a fourth. In fact these profiles are so distinct that the vast majority of couples in each of these categories had similar profiles.

For example, a study of ENRICH (Fowers & Olson, 1989) found that the outcomes of couples who ended up happiest or unhappiest could be distinguished with 85–95% accuracy from their earlier profiles. This is pretty remarkable. It means that ENRICH has very high "predictive validity". In other words, it measures what it claims to measure – marriage. Studies of PREPARE and FOCCUS have found broadly similar results. From this, we can draw two important conclusions:

- We can be really confident that inventories cover the right topics relating to marriage
- We need to be aware that the roots of both good and bad relationship behaviours in the future are found in good

and bad relationship behaviours today. In other words, relationship patterns are hard to change once set.

But there is an important limitation to this. Inventories are not fortune-tellers. They are indeed brilliant at distinguishing between those who do best and those who do worst. The best couples almost always have one kind of profile. The worst almost always have another. The problem is that most couples end up somewhere in the middle. The 1989 study of ENRICH found that you might be 85–95% accurate at distinguishing the best from the worst. But you can do that only when you compare just those two extreme groups to start with. When you start with a more normal mixed group of couples, the accuracy drops to 63–67%. The independent study by Williams and Jurich (1995) found that roughly these same percentages apply to both FOCCUS and PREPARE. That's still remarkable. So you probably still could be a successful fortune-teller using these inventories...just as long as you don't mind being completely wrong about one-third of the couples who come to see you.

Finding 2: Feedback sessions are essential

The second big finding, from a more recent study of PREPARE (Knutson & Olson, 2002), is that couple profiles generally improve if the couple do the inventory a second time immediately following their feedback sessions. In contrast, those who complete the inventory without subsequent feedback do not show such change. PREPARE categorises couples in terms of four profile types – in general rising in a sequence from worst to best. Rather than worry about the names of these types, I'll just number them 1–4. The happiest tend to start with Type 1. The divorced tend to start with Type 4. As with the study of ENRICH discussed above, the predictive validity is worked out backwards rather than forwards and therefore accuracy is once again overstated. Nonetheless, the study found that over half of those not already Type 1 moved up at least one type after feedback. The conclusions we can draw from this are as follows:

- Inventory plus feedback sessions produce a change for the better for most people in the very short term
- Feedback plays an essential part in that change. Simply completing the inventory and discussing it without formal feedback does not have any immediate effect.

Unfortunately the study oversteps the mark by concluding that doing an inventory therefore increases happiness and reduces divorce. If the original couple type today is to retain its accuracy of predicting the state of a relationship tomorrow, any change that happens between now and then is likely to be temporary. You can predict things or you can change things. You can't have both.

Finding 3: Inventories weed out those who are heading for divorce or unhappiness

Inventories also provide couples who might have been set for divorce or unhappiness with enough information to make them realise they are heading for doom. It's important to remember that only they can make that choice, never the support couple or facilitator. Not surprisingly, over 10% of those who take the inventory end up cancelling or postponing their wedding. What I find amazing is that these couples have similar scores and profiles to those who subsequently divorce or who end up unhappy (Fowers & Olson, 1986; Williams & Jurich, 1995).

This is good news. It must be better that a couple go

through heartache now than when they have so much more to lose years later. However, once again we need to be cautious of reading too much into a particular profile to make predictions about future success. Many couples with low profiles will neither divorce nor cancel. Just as a high profile does not guarantee success, nor does a low profile guarantee failure. So we cannot use the profile to tell a couple either to marry or not to marry. They have to figure it out for themselves.

FOCCUS vs PREPARE

FOCCUS and PREPARE have much in common, to their great credit. They are both well researched. They are both comprehensive. They are both very easy to use. They are both relatively easy to get hold of. They are both relatively cheap to use for what they offer. If I wanted to use an inventory, I would take advantage of whichever I could get hold of in my local area. However, if I faced a choice, I would lean marginally in the direction of FOCCUS. Here's why.

One major difference between the two inventories revolves around the ability to categorise couples based on their profiles. Identifying categories is a centrepiece of the extensive research programme undertaken by the PREPARE/ENRICH group (Fowers & Olson, 1992). I have mentioned already that the accuracy of prediction is terrific when you start with happy or divorced couples and look backwards in time at their original categories. Unfortunately, accuracy plummets when you start with the initial category and look forward in time at how the couple end up. That's obviously the way things work in the real world. In my view, therefore, PREPARE overpromotes the benefits of categorising couples more than the research suggests is wise. FOCCUS makes no attempt to distinguish categories or make predictions.

A second difference emerges from the very idea of interpretation and analysis. Using any kind of analysis and interpretation encourages the view that support couples need expertise. Experts dispense wisdom. Experts therefore face raised expectations, from engaged couples and support couples alike, which may or may not be met. Experts also need special training, supervision and monitoring. This is precisely what PREPARE recommends and provides. FOCCUS on the other hand requires minimal expertise, consequently minimal training and no supervision.

For me, FOCCUS's very lack of analysis is a major plus point. Whereas PREPARE makes great play that couple profiles predict couple outcomes, FOCCUS is dismissive of the idea. I agree. The independent evidence is weak and the point is for the couple to discuss their own issues themselves, leading to what FOCCUS calls a "felt need to learn". By enjoying and benefiting from the learning experience the first time, the couple will hopefully seek further learning opportunities.

PREPARE is undoubtedly an excellent programme. I know plenty of people who use it and enjoy it. I especially like the extra practical exercises that make PREPARE a stand-alone programme. My reservation concerns this whole issue of analysis or interpretation and what it implies for potential support couples in terms of training and expertise.

FOCCUS makes its inventory easily accessible to the ordinary couple with minimal training, if any, through inclusion of a list of suggested follow-up questions to accompany each statement. These can be used or not as the support couple sees fit. Follow-up questions are really helpful, especially at first when things can seem a little daunting. It is pretty hard to mess up FOCCUS because the process is so simple. It's also slightly cheaper to use.

FOCCUS sample statements

1. We are in agreement about the husband-and-wife roles each of us expects of the other in our marriage relationship.
2. My future spouse and I seldom differ in our need to talk things out or keep things to ourselves.
3. I am hoping that after marriage my future spouse will change some of his/her behaviours.
4. Sometimes my future spouse feels that I do not listen to him/her.
5. We have discussed the ways our families solve problems and how this may affect our problem-solving.

Copyright, FOCCUS Inc. – Used with permission.

PREPARE sample statements

1. My partner and I have a very close relationship.
2. My partner has some habits I dislike.
3. I can share positive and negative feelings with my partner.
4. We have some important disagreements that never seem to get resolved.
5. We have similar styles of spending and saving.

Copyright, 1998 Life Innovations, Inc.

Summary

Relationship inventories have revolutionised marriage education. Using an inventory is as simple as taking a couple shopping. Inventories are comprehensive lists of statements organised into various topics such as children, communication or personal issues. By providing support couples with such a simple discussion format, mentoring has now come within the reach of any ordinary married couple.

Much excellent research gives us confidence that the inventory is the real expert. Research finds that 85–95% of couples who end up happily married or divorced have particular profiles. However, the caveat is that those with certain profiles won't necessarily end up happily married *or* divorced. While this tells us that inventories are definitely asking the right questions, there is no way of telling whether a couple's profile puts them in a certain category or not. At best, profiles identify risk.

Research also finds that feedback is essential if couples are to benefit from using an inventory. We also know that over 10% of those taking an inventory end up cancelling their weddings. Once again, the profile does not tell them this. They work it out for themselves.

As to which inventory to use, frankly there's not much in it. But, given the choice, I prefer and recommend using the FOCCUS inventory. FOCCUS makes no pretence at analysis or interpretation, in contrast to the equally excellent PREPARE. In this way, responsibility for discussion and solutions remain rightly with the couple. Support-couple expectations and apprehensiveness are thereby minimised. It helps that FOCCUS is also cheaper and easier to use.

Which inventory you use probably matters little in the end. It is because of both these inventories that mentoring has become so accessible to the ordinary married couple.

Selected references
- Fowers, B.J., Montel, K. and Olson, D.H. (1996) Predicting marital success for premarital couple types based on PREPARE. *Journal of Marital and Family Therapy* 22, 103–111.
- Fowers, B.J. and Olson, D.H. (1986) Predicting marital success with PREPARE: A predictive validity study. *Journal of Marital and Family Therapy* 12, 403–413.

- Fowers, B.J. and Olson, D.H. (1989) ENRICH marital inventory: A discriminant validity and cross-validity assessment. *Journal of Marital and Family Therapy* 15, 65–79.
- Fowers, B.J. and Olson, D.H. (1992) Four types of premarital couples: An empirical typology based on PREPARE. *Journal of Family Psychology* 6, 10–21.
- Knutson, L. and Olson, D.H. (2002) Effectiveness of the PREPARE program with premarital couples. From www.lifeinnovations.com
- Williams, L. and Jurich, J. (1995) Predicting marital success after five years: Assessing the predictive validity of FOCCUS. *Journal of Marital and Family Therapy* 21, 141–153.

Full details on FOCCUS, PREPARE and Life Innovations appear in Appendix C.

Chapter 7   # Mentoring in practice

In this chapter

- How to be a good enough support couple
- How to use the FOCCUS inventory
- How to use mentoring flexibly

Good enough support couples

I need to clarify first of all that this chapter explains one particular way of mentoring an engaged or newly-wed couple, using one particular inventory. There are plenty of other ways of mentoring couples. But an inventory provides an easy format to work with and makes sure you cover all the right topics.

For mentoring couples in other situations – e.g. living together, already married, new parents, prisoners due for release, stepfamilies, etc. – you may find other inventories that are more suitable from either of the FOCCUS and PREPARE stables. Of course there's no law that says you have to use an inventory at all to do a great job of mentoring a couple. For example, I mentor couples in crisis without an inventory, but I also have a clear plan to follow.

If you're feeling overwhelmed with things to think about, never fear! So long as you make it clear to your couple that you're not experts, you'll be fine. Using an inventory is virtually idiot-proof. The one I'm going to take you through is practically impossible to mess up. All you have to do is walk your couple slowly through the shopping list of issues and let them do the talking. To make it even easier for you, alongside every subject to discuss comes a list of follow-up questions for the support couples. So if you can't think what to say next, you just have to pick something from the follow-up questions. I'll tell you how to deal with any problems you may face in the next chapter.

The difference between a good enough support couple and an excellent support couple boils down to the way support couples share their experience and the way they gently point out good and bad habits. I've already been through habit-spotting – the bad habits that pull a relationship apart and the good habits that stop the bad habits from happening. This chapter covers how to use an inventory. Maybe you still don't quite believe me when I say mentoring is easy. But it is.

I'll start off by pointing out some ground rules that should be established before mentoring begins: confidentiality, turning up on time, etc. That way everybody knows what to expect and the whole thing will feel safer. Then I'll take you through a typical mentoring session. This usually takes place in the evening, in the support couple's home, with a meal beforehand. There is no reason why this has to happen exactly so. It's up to the support couple and their couple to agree.

If you're mentoring couples who are getting married or are newly-weds, the next thing you need to know is how to use the FOCCUS inventory. You could equally well use the PREPARE inventory, and should do so if it's available near you.

When you receive your FOCCUS folder, its large size can

seem a bit intimidating at first. Once you see how the bits of paper need to be arranged, you'll find that using FOCCUS as a support couple is a doddle. You also need to know that FOCCUS – and indeed PREPARE – is incredibly flexible. You can work your way through as many or as few issues with a couple as you like. It's usually best to discuss with them how many sessions they want to do. Finally, we'll look at what happens afterwards when you've finished. Many support couples and their couples develop deep friendships during the formal part of mentoring.

Ground rules for being a support couple

Before starting mentoring, it's important to have some basic ground rules established. Ground rules allow couples to discuss their personal concerns safely with one another within known boundaries. Ground rules also clarify and set expectations appropriately.

The list below is self-explanatory. You could read through it with your couple or discuss it more generally over the phone beforehand.

- The role of support couples is to facilitate discussion and share experience as necessary
- Support couples should be thought of and treated as extended family members
- Support couples should not be thought of as experts or counsellors
- Couples and support couples must respect private property, wherever mentoring takes place
- Couples and support couples must respect one another and not use mentoring as an excuse to dump

- Couples and support couples must respect timing and aim to start and finish on time as agreed
- Couples and support couples must respect one another's privacy and not probe insensitively
- Couples and support couples must respect confidentiality and not discuss private matters with others
- Support couples reserve the right to seek outside advice on difficult issues.

As a support couple, Kate and I usually discuss these points informally either on the phone beforehand or over dinner at the first meeting.

> *This is what we plan to do on our evenings. We'd like to try and sit down for dinner together as soon as possible after 8. So if you could try to arrive close to 8 o'clock, that would be great. We'll start the questions by 9 and finish by 10.30 unless you are happy with a bit longer. Whatever you tell us stays with us. I hope you'll treat us the same. Don't expect us to be experts. You're going to do the work! We'll just be there to help you through it. Try to think of us as you would think of an uncle and aunt. I'm looking forward to it. It'll be fun!*

The typical support-couple session

The typical support-couple session takes place in the evening, in the support couple's own home, and usually begins with a meal. There is no particular reason other than mutual convenience why evenings are better than any other time. Spending time together is the main thing, whenever that takes place. But it cannot be overemphasised how much impact it has on young couples to be invited for a meal and welcomed into the home of complete strangers. It sends a powerful message that their marriage really must be valuable and important to have all this attention lavished upon it. After all, whoever heard of strangers doing such a thing nowadays?

When Kate and I are mentoring, the way we tend to do it is to invite our couple round to our house for 8pm sharp. By that time we have injected our brood of children into bed and made sure there is some dinner ready. We will have checked with the couple beforehand what sort of thing they like to eat. Dinner is usually something fairly straightforward, such as pasta, Thai curry with rice or fish pie, followed by ice cream. We usually have a bottle of wine with dinner, which helps to break the ice, and we finish with coffee. If the couple offer to bring something along, we suggest they bring some sort of pudding or a bottle of wine.

When we sit down, we find it tends to work best if we seat the couple opposite us. Seating is a surprisingly important issue. Sitting opposite your couple might seem adversarial at first, until you realise that most of the talking is going to be done between husband and wife or fiancé and fiancée, who are now sitting next to each other.

We try to clear all the plates and glasses away by 9pm at the latest so we can start working through the inventory. We will have agreed at the beginning of the evening whether we will finish by 10.30pm or 11pm. Going beyond that is almost always a waste of time. After a day's work, most people are not operating very efficiently once it gets late. I know I'm not. The last thing a support couple needs is a couple thinking about marriage prep. in terms of *"It's OK but it goes on so late…"*

The components of FOCCUS

Mentoring can be done most easily with one of two inventories, PREPARE or FOCCUS, as discussed in the previous chapter. Those who wish to use PREPARE, whether by preference or by local availability, must learn how to use it on one of their training days. Therefore I'm not going to elaborate on how PREPARE should be used. The rest of this chapter is aimed at those wishing to use FOCCUS, which requires little or no training. Contact information for both PREPARE and FOCCUS can be found in Appendix C.

When you get your FOCCUS manual, you will see a large plastic A4 binder that can look quite daunting until you realise how simple it is to use. Instructions in the first section marked **"Introduction"** are very straightforward and easy to understand.

All you really need to know as a support couple are the four main component parts. By opening the manual at the section marked **"Inventory"**, you will find two inventories – one scrambled inventory marked **"Couple Inventory"** (there may be two copies), and one unscrambled inventory marked **"Questions by Categories for Facilitator"**.

1. The **"Couple Inventory"** contains 156 statements in random order. This is followed by a further 33 statements in three special sections. These are for "Interfaith Marriages", "Second Marriage Couples" and "Cohabiting Couples". Each special section is there because it refers to couples at a known higher risk of divorce.

2. The **"Questions by Categories for Facilitator"** inventory unscrambles the 156 statements and reorganises them neatly into thirteen "categories" and three "summary

categories". The thirteen categories include themes such as "Lifestyle Expectations", "Communication", "Financial Issues" and "Sexuality Issues". The three summary categories each take a representative cross section of statements from the entire inventory that covers "Key Problem Indicators", "Family of Origin" and "Dual Careers".

Before the couple start their mentoring sessions, each of them needs to have worked through the **"Couple Inventory"** and completed a separate **"Answer Sheet"**, which will usually be at the back of the manual. All the couple do on their separate sheets is say whether they **Agree**, **Disagree** or are **Uncertain** about each statement. Completion of the inventory by the couple is easiest on line via www.foccus.co.uk, which makes things very easy. Outside the UK, contact www.foccusinc.com.

If done on paper, answers are then sent off for processing. There are instructions for where to send them at the front of the manual. Processing usually takes up to a week. Relationship organisations will usually do all this on behalf of their support couples.

3. The processed **"Couple Report"** is available immediately on line to the support couple. Paper copies will otherwise be sent back within a few days. A sample of this is shown in Figure 7.1. The cover page starts with a summary of demographic details: the couple's respective age, education, income, ethnicity, marital status, religion, etc. All you are looking for here is areas of difference. Is the man much older than the woman? Is the woman earning much more than the man? Is she better educated? Do they have different religions? Big differences represent areas of potential conflict that you will need to watch out for.

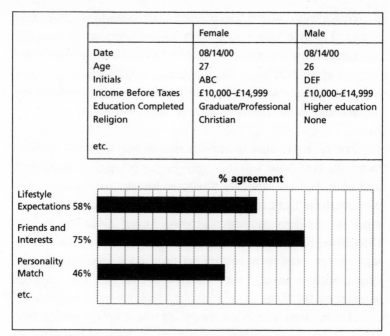

Figure 7.1 FOCCUS Couple Report, page 1

Below this is a fancy-looking chart telling you how much the couple agree with each other on each category. Beware! This information is less useful than it looks. All it really tells you is whether you are going to have to work hard with a couple and on which categories. As a rule of thumb, scores above 60% mean easier issues to work through. Scores below 60% usually mean more difficult issues to work through. That's it!

I choose not to show a couple the front page of their report, at least at first. There is no reason why they should ask for it unless they know it exists. Of course I would show it if asked. However, there are good reasons for delaying this until session 2 or 3.

If a couple have very high scores, they could become overconfident. I'd rather they did some work first so that I can encourage them further by showing them how much they are in accord. Likewise, a couple with low scores could get easily discouraged. I usually wait until after a particularly good category or session to show them the chart. *"Look how you originally agreed on so little. But the way you have worked through this last category shows you can do really well together. Keep going, guys. I'm impressed."*

Over the page, you then have a list of the couple's responses, broken down category by category, statement by statement. For example, the first category is called "**Lifestyle Expectations**". Each statement then has six columns. Column 1 gives the number of the statement. Columns 2 and 3 show how the Male and Female responded. Column 4 shows the preferred answer to that statement. Columns 5 and 6 present the same information in a different way. If all three answers concur, a summary of the statement will be found in the column "**Areas of Agreement**". If not, it will go in the column "**Areas of Disagreement**".

I usually circle the responses that do not match the preferred answer, as I have done on the example in Figure 7.2. That shows me at a glance whether the man or the woman

Lifestyle Expectations					
#	M	F	Preferred	Areas of Disagreement	Areas of Agreement
6	A	(D)	A	Agreement on roles in marriage	
57	D	D	D		Concern growing up affect roles
21	(U)	A	A	Content with way we manage home	
51	D	D	D		Background causes house problems

Figure 7.2 FOCCUS Couple Report, page 2

disagrees most. Usually it's a mix. Very occasionally there is a major imbalance. In that case, I'd simply make a mental note that one of the couple may be very much more uncertain than the other about their decision to marry.

4. Finally, you need to open up the manual to the section marked "**Content Categories**". Here you will find three pages of information on each of the thirteen categories. The first page covers the first category, "**Lifestyle Expectations**". There is a short summary of what this category is all about. Underneath is a bit about patterns. This gives an idea of how the category is subdivided into patterns of behaviour. Over the page is the secret weapon for support couples: follow-up questions. Don't worry about the scary title at the top that starts "**Facilitator Aids...**" Beside every statement is a list of possible questions you can choose to use, or not, to help the couple talk. This makes mentoring really easy. If you're stuck, ask a follow-up question.

The mechanics of mentoring using FOCCUS

So now that you know the various bits of FOCCUS, I will explain how to use them. First of all, Kate and I sit ourselves opposite our couple across the kitchen table. Remember that the purpose of this is that they can talk unobstructed to one another. We may even encourage them to turn their chairs towards each other. We give them the scrambled "**Couple Inventory**", a pen and some paper for notes. We hang on to the "**Couple Report**", the unscrambled inventory and the "**Follow-up Questions**". Whoever is going to direct operations takes the "**Couple Report**". In our house I'm the control freak, so that's me. Kate is the more sensible one who throws

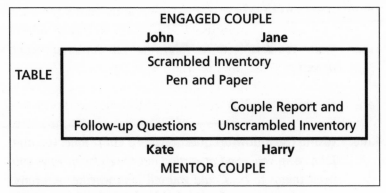

Figure 7.3 Suggested table layout for mentoring

out interesting questions that illuminate the issue. So she gets the follow-up questions.

All you need to know now is how to go through each statement. Since the process is the same each time, when you know how to go through one statement, then you know how to do all of them. This is roughly what the process sounds like:

Harry: *"We're going to start with a section called 'Lifestyle Expectations'. This covers what you expect from your marriage as a result of what you've experienced growing up. John's expectations of the perfect marriage may be quite different from Jane's. So these questions will shed some light on where you agree and where you disagree. John, would you start by reading out Question 6 to Jane?"*

John: (reads) *"We are in agreement about the husband-and-wife roles each of us expects of the other in our marriage relationship."*

Harry: *"Thank you. John, you agreed with this. Jane, you disagreed. John, tell Jane what you thought you had agreed."*

John: (explains to Jane)

Harry: *"Jane, you disagreed. Tell John what you think you hadn't agreed."*

Jane: (explains to John)

Kate: (using the follow-up questions as a cue) *"Jane, you and John seem very good at sorting out the different ways you want things to be. Could you tell John whether you have any non-negotiables, any roles you either definitely want or definitely don't want?"*

Jane: (explains to John)

Kate: *"And what about you, John? Tell Jane whether you have any non-negotiables."*

John: (explains to Jane)

Harry: *"Great. That sounds very encouraging. Jane, would you now read Question 57 to John, please...."*

You may have noted some important principles even from this short dialogue.

1. **Being a support couple means being directive.** It is not non-directive, like counselling. I think of the role of the support couple as a bit like that of traffic police. There are so many questions to get through. You simply have to direct the couple actively through the traffic jam of questions so that they get to look at as many topics as possible. Raising awareness of issues is much more important

than having to explore and solve every issue. Raising awareness is your job. Exploring and solving is theirs.

2. **Being a support couple means being non-expert.** Once again, it is not like counselling. The key relationships are engaged man to engaged woman and support-couple husband to wife. There is no need for opinions, advice, counselling or psychotherapy. That means support couples do not need expert skills. Reflecting skills are fine for one-to-one counselling, but not for marriage. However, there is scope for teaching and reinforcing relationship principles, such as those in the previous chapters on Good and Bad Habits.

3. **Being a support couple means facilitating.** The couple do the talking and the work. Note that in the example above the support couple keep saying *"tell John..."* or *"tell Jane..."* If you don't do this, John and Jane will naturally speak to the person who asked the question. I find I usually have to tell a couple three or four times before they get the message. Like a traffic policeman, I will wave my arms to show how they should talk to each other and not to me. Once they have got into the habit of doing this, it will also help prevent the support couple from slipping into expert mode to solve their problems for them.

4. **Being a support couple means sharing.** When a couple come up with a completely wacky comment, it's very tempting to tell them they've got it wrong. Beware! Once you move into the world of opinions, you're on dodgy ground. Winning an argument becomes irrelevant if you ruin the relationship in the process. The far better way to highlight dodgy thinking is to share your own experi-

ence, talking more to each other if possible than to the couple. For example:

Harry: *"The first time that happened to us, we ended up completely blowing it because of... Do you remember that?"* (he asks, turning to Kate)

Kate: *"I think the less said the better. It's a miracle I married you after what you said to that nice waiter..."* (she turns back to the couple) *"Would you believe this supposedly intelligent man..."* etc., etc.

With luck, the couple will be more open to learning from a principle illustrated in a story – which is often more amusing in hindsight than it seemed at the time. They can relate better to that personally than to a principle rammed down their throats whether they want it or not.

5. **Being a support couple is easy.** Support couples really only have to accompany a couple through the inventory, category by category, statement by statement. Go back to the supermarket analogy I gave earlier. All you have to do is imagine you're the store manager. You walk them up each aisle and point out items one by one. *"What about apples?"* say the support couple. *"I like them,"* says the man. *"I can't stand them,"* says the woman. *"Oh, I had always assumed you did like them. There's no reason we have to buy them. What shall we get instead?"* They then happily agree to buy pears. All the support couple did was point at fruit. What could be easier!

It is very important to try and keep things light-hearted. You will sometimes find the FOCCUS statements become complicated to understand. *"We often disagree that we feel uncertain about..."* Try saying you disagree with that one and then work out what you meant! Double negatives and triple negatives are all too difficult. When that happens, laugh it off! It really doesn't matter if you don't understand the question. Move on to the next one. Alternatively, you can help a couple to rephrase what they said. For example: *"You said you disagreed that you feel uncertain. So what you mean is that you* do *feel certain!"*

Fitting mentoring to the couple

I hope you can now see how incredibly easy mentoring is. Doubts and reservations that people have beforehand usually stem from the belief that *"we aren't good enough"* or *"we haven't much to offer"* or *"I just don't believe it's that easy"*. The reason I resist all attempts at professionalising mentoring is that it reinforces the mistaken belief that you have to be a professional. It leads us back to thinking about problems and experts. These concerns are almost always dispelled by the reality of mentoring. *"It was so much easier than I expected"* is a very common response. One pastor's wife told me, after finishing mentoring their first couple, *"I wasn't sure whether I felt well trained after your mentor-training course. But after mentoring a couple, I knew I had been."*

There are lots of ways of doing mentoring with an inventory. This is a flexible process. Ideally, a couple need to know some basic skills beforehand. Many UK support couples will be part of a Community Family Trust or a church course that teaches this. If not, the support couple can easily run through the principles outlined in Chapters 3, 4 and 5 – Bad Habits, Good Habits and Party Tricks. If that seems a daunting prospect, don't worry. Simply get the couple to read these chapters themselves before they come to you for mentoring. Then all you have to do is reinforce those skills by getting the couple to use them as the occasion demands. Armed with these few simple skills, the inventory provides a structured pathway for a couple to work through the issues that are relevant to them.

Let's get back to how to get through it all. 156 statements divided into six sessions of 90 minutes gives you an average of 3 $1/2$ minutes per statement. That sounds pretty tough to me. Fewer evenings means even less time or fewer statements!

The answer is that you don't have to get through everything. Kate and I have actually finished the entire inventory only twice out of thirteen engaged couples we have mentored to date. Both couples were spectacularly wonderful, had few areas of contention, communicated these differences beautifully, and almost certainly didn't need mentoring. The funny thing, though, is that they loved the course and said they had benefited from it greatly.

There is a strong case for doing more than two sessions. Research studies in the US show that people recall their marriage preparation up to four years later if it had an optimum five to seven sessions. One to two sessions have little or no impact. The same applies at the other end, if you do more than twelve sessions. I therefore suggest a minimum of three and a maximum of six sessions, during which support couples cover as much ground as they can. More than six sessions suggests to me that the support couple are probably becoming counsellors.

The way Kate and I manage this task is to aim to get through between one and three categories per session. We almost always spend the entire first evening meandering slowly through the first category, *"Lifestyle Expectations"*. This is a terrific subject that touches on just about everything else

	Session	Categories Covered
Typical	1	Lifestyle Expectations
	2	Friends and Interests, Personality Match
	3	Personal Issues, Communication, Problem-Solving
	4	Sexuality, Financial, Readiness
Full Programme	1	Lifestyle Expectations
	2–6	Two or three categories each session
Fast Track	1	Lifestyle Expectations
	2	Key Problem Indicators

Figure 7.4 How many FOCCUS sessions?

that is likely to come up in subsequent categories. The couple enjoy the freedom to roam and are usually encouraged to discover how much they agree. Where they didn't agree, they are often encouraged to discover that the same thing also happened to their support couple and that disagreements do not have to be the end of the world. The very rare occasions when major issues have cropped up later on for us involved *"personal issues"* – drugs, sex and alcohol – or *"parenting"* – children. After such a thorough discussion of expectations, it is very often the case that in subsequent categories a statement will be read out to which the reply is: *"We've already dealt with that. Next!"*

Our typical couple get four sessions. The first evening covers the first category. We then usually show the couple the front-page chart in order to encourage them. We let them decide which categories to discuss next, bearing in mind that the categories generally work best in the order they are presented, if possible. That usually allows us to cover two categories an evening thereafter for three more evenings. So we end up completing around seven of the thirteen categories in total.

There are many other ways to do this. The support couple could simply take the couple through the "**Summary Category**" called "**Key Problem Indicators**". In the "**Couple Report**", you will see an asterisk marked against two or three statements in each category. These are the "**Key Problem Indicators**" for that category. If you only wanted to choose two or three statements per category, these would be the important ones to pick. In the manual, these statements are grouped together in the "**Summary Categories**" section under "**Key Problem Indicators**". That's where you find the follow-up questions.

Alternatively, you could choose a handful of statements per category and run through those. Or you could just pick the statements where the couple disagree. You can see how flexible it is. It's up to the four of you to choose how to do it, depending on time available, inclination and how much you're all enjoying the process.

What do you do when the couple talk forever and you begin to worry how you will ever finish the first category, let alone half a dozen? The answer is to give the couple a pen and paper. If they go on and on, be direct: *"May I suggest you write this subject down and talk about it more between the two of you?"*

Let me finish with a short story about what happened when Kate and I mentored our most recent couple. This couple were articulate, highly lucid and generally wonderful together. We had just one evening with them because they were moving to another city and wanted something rather than nothing. After completing "**Lifestyle Expectations**", Kate and I were both feeling we had contributed little as a support couple. They were already pretty clued up. We showed them the FOCCUS profile and asked what they'd like to talk about in the remaining half hour. The girl asked to cover the section on religion because she was searching spiritually and thought it might become important to her. Her fiancé was tolerant of this but clearly not interested in participating. What would it be like, we asked, if she did get into God in a big way? Suddenly we had opened up a huge issue that could become a major problem for them if they didn't discuss it. As they left our house, Kate and I felt very smug that we had done our job properly. We had raised a hidden issue that they simply hadn't dared discuss. The inventory made it easy for us.

Formal and informal mentoring

Not very long ago, Kate and I were going through a sticky patch in our marriage. Being pregnant with our sixth child probably didn't help matters much. One evening we were sitting in the car on our way to London for dinner with friends. It should have been a wonderful time away from the kids. Instead, we argued all the way to London. We had a very nice smiley dinner with our friends. Then we argued all the way back to Bristol. By 1 o'clock in the morning, we were all argued out. This is an especially embarrassing situation to be in as I'm supposed to teach communication skills. Ha! What a joke. If I can't practise what I preach at home, what right do I have to teach it? It obviously doesn't work. You get the idea of what I was feeling. Well, when we woke up in the morning we continued arguing. During a lull in the storm, we managed to find something we could agree about. We needed to do something about our arguing.

Later that morning I rang some friends of ours, called Arthur and Jenny. They had been informal mentors to us since we had returned to the UK from living overseas. I rather gingerly picked up the phone and dialled. Jenny answered.

"Help, Jenny," I squeaked. *"Can we come over and see you? We're just not communicating very well."*

With great grace and wisdom, she replied, *"Harry, I'm sure you know what you should be doing. You teach it. Of course you can come over if you want. But I just want to ask you one question. Are you making time for one another?"* Oops, I thought immediately. That was it. Time. Sure enough, the next evening, Kate and I sat down on our bed and chatted for hours. Our communication worked like magic and our marriage was back on the up-cycle.

This is an example of exceptionally brilliant but very simple informal mentoring. Having Jenny and Arthur in the background has felt to us like having a safety net. I may well know a great deal about research on marriage and marriage education. But there really is no substitute for their long experience of marriage. I look to them because of their experience. What Jenny reminded me was that it is impossible to communicate well when you're not feeling valued. Time equals value for Kate. That's one of her love languages. So all the communication skills in the world wouldn't have meant a thing as long as I wasn't giving Kate time.

When you finish the formal mentoring with a couple, this is the kind of role you could have as a support couple. You are simply there in the background as friends, a source of support and gentle words of wisdom offered rather than thrust. Kate and I didn't have serious problems when I called Jenny. But we knew we were going through a bad patch. You can be there for your couple when that happens. Or you could walk away from your couple after the formal mentoring finishes. It's a free choice.

In turn, Kate and I have mentored thirteen engaged couples in the last four years. We stay in touch with most of them. Keeping in touch is good fun. We sometimes have dinner with couples who live near us – say, once a year. Or I might e-mail them unexpectedly. Always, the connection is a positive and tender one. There are good memories of a positive experience to fall back on. When we meet up with a couple, we can talk about their relationship or just enjoy an evening together. We're just there if they need us. That's informal mentoring. Of course it's quite possible that none of them will speak to us again after they've read what basket cases we can be. But they knew that already.

Whether as a support couple you continue a friendship with your couple informally is not really that important. The most important thing is that your couple have learned that it's OK to talk. So if you do decide not to stay in contact, or can't because either of you are moving, encourage your couple to get friendly with some other married couple to whom they can chat informally about their marriage.

Summary

Good enough mentoring starts with some sensible ground rules to set expectations. Everybody needs to know that things like timing and confidentiality are important. Thereafter the process of mentoring is simple. The process described in this chapter applies particularly to engaged or newly-wed couples. But you can adapt the broad principles for mentoring couples at all sorts of stages of life.

The typical process involves spending several sessions with a couple, usually in the evening, usually at the support couple's home, and usually preceded by dinner and wine to break the ice. This may be too difficult for some. The important thing is to provide the time to talk couple to couple.

What to do in the evenings is made easy with an inventory. You can use FOCCUS or PREPARE – whichever is available locally. FOCCUS is available on line as well as being a bit cheaper and easier to use. Using PREPARE requires that you do their course. Either is fine. In this chapter, therefore, I've only outlined how to use FOCCUS.

Once you've understood the mechanics of how to arrange the component parts of FOCCUS, the rest is easy. At least a week before mentoring begins, the couple will each have completed **Answer Sheets** where they say they **Agree**, **Disagree** or are **Uncertain** about each of 156 statements and special sections. This can also be done on line. The answer sheets are then sent for processing and returned a few days later as the **Couple Report**.

All the support couple need is the **Couple Report**, an unscrambled copy of the **Inventory**, and a list of **Follow-up Questions** found in the **Summary Category** section of the FOCCUS manual. All the couple need is a scrambled copy of the **Inventory**, a pen and some paper for notes. If this sounds confusing, it's not when you put the bits of paper on the table in front of you. Support couples need do no preparation and do not need to take notes.

Going through a single statement is very straightforward. The couple read it out. You tell them what they said. *"John, you agreed. Jane, you disagreed."* They then talk to each other about what they meant. You have a list of follow-up questions to keep the discussion going if you need them. How they answered at the time isn't terribly important. The key is to get them talking. You can then sit back and enjoy their discussion. Where there are patterns to spot, both good and bad, you can gently point them out. Where your experience is relevant, you can sensitively share it. Then you move them on to the next statement and repeat the process.

Working through thirteen categories, each with a dozen or so statements, can seem a lot. It did to me when I started.

But the process is flexible and you don't have to do everything. Usually the first category, "Lifestyle Expectations", covers most of the major issues. That takes much or all of the first evening. You then find that you can whistle through subsequent categories much faster, two or three per evening, because the major issues have already been discussed at length. Which categories you discuss and how many sessions you take can be discussed openly with your couple.

When you've done all you want, you can part there and then. Alternatively, you can continue as informal mentors or friends. You might have an informal dinner together once a year. You might otherwise be there in the background for them as a well-informed uncle and aunt figure. Either way you've done a great job.

The time you spent with that couple starting out will have shown them the value of their marriage. They will also have seen that it's OK to learn and OK to talk. Bottling it all up and thinking they're on their own can lead couples to doom. Chatting with a friend who is on the side of their marriage will nip problems in the bud. It works for me!

Chapter 8 **Knowing our limits**

In this chapter

- How to deal with arguments
- How to deal with couple issues – cohabitation, sex and money
- How to deal with individual issues – mental and physical health

When things go wrong

So what happens when things go horribly wrong? Kate and I sometimes feel quite helpless when some awful or deep problem crops up. What should we do? Help! I'm a support couple; get me out of here.

Let's say we welcome a couple into our house for their second evening with us. The atmosphere between them seems heavy and they appear closed to each other. We sit down to dinner and a blazing row breaks out. Or, as we cover the section on sexuality, our newly-wed couple start talking about their lack of sex life together. They seem to find it very much easier to talk about sex than we do. They're looking to us for advice. Or, as we talk with our couple, it becomes fairly obvious that one of them is very poor at expressing themselves, or appears easily withdrawn and depressed, or has a history of drug or alcohol abuse, or a memory of child abuse. What do we do? How do we handle the situation?

I hope this chapter will give you some reassurance about dealing with difficult issues. There is one major principle involved that keeps us on track – as it will you. As a support couple, we are here as well-informed uncles and aunts. No more. No less. Uncles and aunts do not know the answer to everything. We are ordinary people who have the best interests of our couple at heart. Therefore we do not have to be responsible for solving their difficult issues. However, as well-informed people, we know a little about many subjects. That does not make us experts. We need only know our own limits and where to go next.

I want to look at three major areas. The first of these is rows or arguments. These are usually the easiest to deal with. Stopping a row usually involves being very direct but also very affirming to both. You may need to have a cooling-off period before anything else can happen. But, to get the couple talking constructively again, it's largely a matter of applying the simple skills you learned in the earlier chapters.

The second is issues affecting the couple. Sex, cohabitation and money can be intimidating subjects. They both cause and reflect underlying concerns and needs. Having a few basic facts and ideas up your sleeve can help a lot here. Ultimately, pointing the couple at their GP or a specialist book is the most responsible way ahead.

The third is issues especially affecting one individual. There is a whole bunch of horrors here, ranging from depression and insecurity to drug and alcohol abuse, or a history of child abuse. I'll give you a bit of practical information on some of these subjects. But in the main the best course of action is either to send the couple off to discuss things on their own or to suggest the person affected considers getting one-to-one counselling.

Difficult issues are really only difficult for support couples when we see ourselves in the role of experts. We are not experts. We do not have to have clever answers. We are merely well-informed extended family members. We need only to know our limits and to stop when we reach those limits. Difficult issues are therefore difficult for the couple and not for us. With this guiding principle at the front of our minds, let me take you through these three difficult areas I have highlighted.

Arguments

The first difficult area is arguments or rows. Many people instinctively flinch away from rows. It's hardly surprising. Conflict can be very painful and unpleasant to watch. Conflict in others may remind us of previous rows that we have had ourselves. When a couple start blowing each other to bits in a row, how should we handle the situation as support couples?

Let me backtrack a bit and summarise the practical stuff I covered in Chapters 3, 4 and 5 on Bad Habits, Good Habits and Party Tricks. The biggest key to a successful marriage is to reduce the negative ways we handle differences. We want to relate less destructively (fewer bad habits) and more constructively (more good habits). Part of this therefore involves learning how to recognise our bad habits – such as Scoring Points, Thinking the Worst, Opting Out or Putting Down. Part of it involves learning how to use good habits to stop us hurting one another – communicating constructively and then accepting or resolving our differences. Part may also involve learning how to use party tricks to help us work with our differences.

All support couples need to know is how to identify the bad habits or STOP signs, how to coach a couple through basic paraphrase and problem-solving skills, and how to discuss and apply one of the party tricks. None of this is especially difficult for the average married couple. You don't need to be an expert to know it or coach it. It definitely comes under the category of being well informed.

If and when a row breaks out, I tend to let it run on a bit in the hope that the couple will stop arguing and recognise they need to do things better for themselves. Sometimes one person will make a repair attempt – *"Come on, can't we sort this out? Hey, we're getting married. We love each other!"* etc. How the other person responds to this is very important. As a support couple, when a repair attempt is rejected, you need to point it out fast. *"John, hang on a second, what has Jane just said to you? She's trying to reach out and make up with you. You need to tell her what you've heard her say."*

As the row develops, you must interrupt the destructive pattern at some point in order to model to them a way out. Automatic patterns of behaviour get established very quickly. She does this. He does that. She responds. He responds. A pattern is established. Your job is to tell them to stop, ask them to tell you what pattern is happening – or tell them if they can't work it out – and then get them to listen to each other using paraphrases.

After telling them to stop, you may need to give them time to cool down. Remember HALT – Hungry, Angry, Lonely, Tired. It's hard to communicate when you are wound up. But you'll often find that gently coaching them through paraphrasing will start to melt the ice and may even bring out deeper issues and real understanding.

So the argument is brewing. Kate and I let it brew. One of us will then spot a misunderstanding or escalation and use that as a cue to interrupt. *"Whoa, whoa, whoa. Stop, stop, stop. Come on, guys. This is not going well right now. Remember the STOP signs. What's the pattern that's developing here?"* Hopefully they will spot their put-downs, or whatever pattern it is. Then one of us will suggest the following: *"OK. Let's go back to what Jane has to say. Then I want you, John, to paraphrase back what you heard. This is a good time to use paraphrasing. Jane, I think you had something important there to tell John. So off you go. Tell John again."*

I was coaching an engaged couple on a pre-marriage course and they were discussing what to do with an imaginary windfall voucher from a travel agent – what would be their dream holiday. The idea of the exercise was simply to communicate and acknowledge their differences and not to agree on where to go. The guy went first, telling of his dream holiday filled with action and adventure. When they swapped roles, the girl sounded a bit defensive and closed as she tentatively talked of lounging by a swimming pool and having the odd facial. He paraphrased this back to her as *"So what you'd really like on your holiday is to be pampered"*. She was astonished that he was so perceptive. *"I wanted to say that so much but after what you said you wanted, I didn't dare."* Watching her face light up was like watching a rose bloom. A good paraphrase by an attentive listener can give a tremendous lift to a relationship. So don't underestimate the power of paraphrase in its context – which is to deal with difficult issues.

It may be that your couple are still unwilling or unable to communicate constructively with each other. That is where you might be able to introduce one of the party tricks very effectively. If they are badly miscommunicating and not accepting each other as different, then try Love Languages or Emotional Needs. *"You guys are so different. And that's OK.*

Everybody is. I wonder if you've heard about the idea of Love Languages? It might help you here."

Where a fairly obvious pattern of behaviour is repeating itself, try using The Dance. You'll all need to stand up to do this. *"Come over here, guys. Believe it or not...we are going to teach you how to dance!"* That unexpected change in setting and humour can help clear the air. Most importantly, of course, you need to be very clear beforehand that you know how the dance works, how to translate real-life behaviour into moves, and how to work through alternative moves. The Dance can be very powerful in helping understanding and in finding a possible solution. Don't be surprised to see your arguing couple hugging each other in tears just a few minutes later.

Couple issues

Cohabitation

At a time when the cultural norm is to live together before getting married, or even just to live together, it may seem prudish and irrelevant even to raise the subject of cohabitation as an issue. Many people will also regard this as merely an outdated religious issue. Yet it's not. In Chapter 10 I'm going to talk in more detail about some of the many differences found by researchers between those who live together with or without marrying. Most importantly, cohabiting without plans to marry raises your risk of subsequent divorce when you do marry by some 40–85%.

My approach to this is to make sure that the subject does come up. FOCCUS includes a special section on the subject precisely because it does raise the risks. Your couple are there in front of you in order to give their marriage the best chance.

Cohabiting is a matter that needs to be addressed. As a support couple, your main task on this topic is to ask the couple about their motives for cohabiting and for getting married and what they expect to change as a result.

Realistically, the couple are not going to respond positively to well-meaning advice not to cohabit at all. It just sounds silly. What I do is make sure they know that the risks are much higher for them if they don't do something about it. The most likely reason is to do with the attitude change and subsequent behaviour change that comes with getting married. For those who have lived together with one eye on the short-term option of getting out if things don't work, it might be more difficult to make the transition to a lifelong commitment where their options are more limited. The couple are still living together. But have they made that mental shift from short-term "options-open" to long-term "options-closed"? Cohabitation commitment tends to be based on a conditional contract – I will stay if certain conditions are met. Marriage commitment is based on an unconditional promise – I will stay regardless.

My gentle recommendation is therefore to suggest that couples live apart before their wedding day – for a week, two weeks, a month, two months or whatever they can manage. In that way, the couple will be more likely to see their wedding day and night as the beginning of a new relationship and not just a continuation of the old one. That will give them a stronger sense of commitment to putting more effort into the marriage and sticking things out when times get tough, as they will. Couples are not completely closed to this idea but they may need practical help. For example, some friends of mine put up the fiancée they were mentoring in their own home for a month before her wedding so their couple could enter married life as a new relationship.

One other important issue you may want to raise with cohabiting couples is how they manage their money. A study (Heimdal & Houseknecht, 2003) of couples in both Sweden and the US found that while most first-time married couples have joint accounts, most cohabiting couples and previously divorced couples have separate accounts. No other economic or social factors could explain this phenomenon. Do you suppose that those who live together are keeping their escape routes open – just in case? Do you suppose that those who have had a previous divorce are also keeping their escape routes open – just in case? We wonder why break-up rates are so very much higher among cohabiting couples and second marriages. Separate bank accounts today sow the seeds of separation tomorrow – as do pre-nuptial agreements...but that's another story. If the couple aren't planning a joint bank account, I would challenge them to discuss what would happen if they did.

Sex

So what do I know about sex? After all, I'm just a married father – of six children, admittedly. But I've read around a bit, I know enough to be dangerous and I know where to look for answers! That's all a support couple have to know.

The mechanics of sex are all around us – in films, on TV, in magazines, in top tips, etc. The bravado and aggressive confidence with which this is projected can build up unrealistic expectations in us of how it should be and how often we should have it. Yet it is still quite difficult to talk openly about the real intimate details of how often we have sex, what we like, what we don't like, what feels great and what hurts. So to sit down with another couple you hardly know and talk about sex can take some guts! I know, having done it both ways – so to speak.

Sex is endlessly cited as one of the major reasons for divorce, whether too little sex or sex outside the marriage. Yet, in reality, sex is more like the barometer of a marriage and not the cause of its success or failure. So many other factors are involved – beliefs about what is normal, what we think of ourselves and our bodies, the quality of our marital relation-ship, the availability of other potential partners, our previous sexual history, our family history, etc. Sex may often be the reason given for divorce. But just as divorce reflects what has gone before, so does sex.

It may therefore help support couples to be aware of some basic information that is not always well known. Sex problems do crop up among the engaged and newly-weds. Knowing how to handle them as a support couple is all about knowing our own limits. For example, I know how to talk couples through confidence crises and how to give them a basic plan – which I'll talk about below. But I also know I am no expert. I know a few books that can help people and I know that it's worth suggesting couples see their GP to rule out the possibility of medical problems.

Concerning how often, US sex expert Barry McCarthy says that one in five married couples have sex less than once a month and a further one in five couples have sex less than twice a month. The average is apparently somewhere between two and fifteen times a month. For about 40% of couples, both spouses are satisfied with this. Among the remainder, it is usually the case that one spouse is satisfied and one dissatisfied.

Low-sex marriages may simply boil down to tiredness and stress with work and children. Michele Weiner-Davis, author of *The Sex-Starved Marriage*, says that unfulfilled expec-tations are also largely to blame. Getting round to sex is therefore the key problem for most couples, rather than sex itself. Where spouses have different desires, she recommends different strategies for the high- and low-desire spouse. The high-desire spouse should talk about what it's like *"when you say no"* and try to do more of the little things that make their spouse happy – be a friend. The low-desire spouse should try to make sex a bigger priority, flirt a bit, and just do it – you may not feel like it when you start, but you will by the time you get going! For a support couple faced with such a problem, this sounds like a sensible starting point.

Where anxiety is concerned, one of the most commonly recommended programmes is called "Sensate Focus". This exercise involves putting a temporary ban on sex for a limited time in order to explore touch alone. The first part of the exercise involves each spouse individually and privately spending time exploring their own body – what it looks like, what feels nice, what doesn't. The second part involves taking turns in touching each other – without touching the genitals and without having sex. Not having to have sex during this time can take away a lot of the anxiety in itself. More details of this can be found easily enough on the Internet, e.g. on the BBC web site. I hope that the unintentionally awful name "Sensate Focus" will help you laugh your way through the programme. Maybe the name wasn't so unintentional after all...

As far as affairs go, the late sex expert Shirley Glass said that a surprisingly large minority of married people commit adultery, most often with workplace colleagues. Figures for adultery vary tremendously from study to study, so there is no definitive answer other than to say it probably affects up to a third of married people. Protecting a marriage against infidelity in the workplace may be very important for some couples.

A newly-wed couple I know well told the husband's employer that he would no longer be sharing long work shifts with female staff. The wife was rightly concerned that her husband would have been spending more time alone with young single girls than with his wife! Infidelity can happen to anyone. Limiting opportunities is one way to reduce the risk. Glass's view is that where affairs do happen, the only way through is to talk about the gory details. A third of marriages may not survive infidelity but talking about it deromanticises the myth and can help rebuild intimacy. Adultery is often never detected and spouses will often behave well and have a good sex life at home while being unfaithful.

Money

What do I know about money? Hopefully a bit more than I know about sex, as I used to be a partner in a small stock-broking firm in Asia! One of the reasons we were successful among our far bigger competitors was that we helped our clients understand basic investment and valuation principles. Yes, even the professionals aren't always as hot as you might like to think. Once you break through the absurd protective jargon that fills the weekend financial pages, managing money at home also relies on some simple principles.

Not surprisingly, money is another widely cited cause of divorce. Yet, just as with sex, it's more often the outcome of problems than the cause of them. So much is written about money and debt management that I'm not going to go into it in great detail. Ask a friend if you want to know how to budget. Suffice to say I have some basic rules of thumb that have yet to let me down.

1. *Firstly, understand that money is far more than just a commodity for most people.* It can represent value – i.e. I see money as something to be stored and gathered over time. It can represent identity – i.e. I am somebody if I

have money. It can represent expectations – i.e. I expect a certain lifestyle. It can represent security – i.e. I need money to feel secure. Very often it also represents power and control – i.e. I have the chequebook so I am beholden to nobody. Support couples can add a great deal of value to a couple simply by getting them to talk about and acknowledge these different perceptions. What does money mean to you?

2. *Secondly, acknowledge and talk about our different attitudes to money.* That doesn't mean we have to resolve all our differences. Kate and I have wildly different attitudes to money. I tend to think of money as a commodity to be used when necessary. Kate tends to think of money as something to be built up over time as a measure of our success in life. One of the ways we have learned to resolve this is by keeping track of our spending and agreeing significant new expenses beforehand together. We work as a team.

3. *Thirdly, keep track of our family budget by dividing it into fixed and variable income and expenses.* "Fixed" should include things like mortgage, salary, tax, utilities, insurance. These are outside our control. "Variable" should include things like supermarket bills, entertainment, petrol, Christmas gifts, holidays. These are inside our control. For most people, income is largely fixed. For budgeting I recommend starting by knocking off 10% of income for saving. This is the family pension fund and not to be used for other purposes. Some will think knocking off a further proportion for charitable giving is also wise. Thereafter, our variable expenses are simply what's left after the fixed expenses. This is an exercise that a

support couple can easily do with their couple if necessary. It can be a real eye-opener.

4. *Fourthly, avoid credit cards at all costs.* There are no cheap credit cards. Consumer debt holds endless families to ransom. The promise of a new DVD or a holiday today may give us temporary satisfaction. But at extortionate interest rates of 10–20% we end up paying well over the odds in the long run. It's cheaper, safer, wiser and more satisfying to wait and delay our gratification. Rule one of any debt-reduction programme must be to get rid of credit-card debts first – because they are the most expensive. Anyone who ever comes to me for money advice gets told to cut up their credit cards now and throw them away. I usually prefer to do it right then, on the spot. I also recommend tearing up the junk mail sent by rapacious banks and returning it to them in their own prepaid envelopes.

5. *Fifthly, and finally, give ourselves room for manoeuvre.* Taking on the maximum mortgage and/or credit-card debt that I can afford now leaves me at huge risk. When interest rates rise by 1%, our interest bill doesn't go up by just 1%. It's leveraged. In other words, the bill goes up a lot more. A few years ago, some newly-weds came to ask my advice about a house they wanted to do up and split in two. By selling the other half, they reckoned they could reduce the cost of their own half. I told them I thought they risked over-extending themselves by doubling their mortgage. I suggested that, by living more within their means, they would enjoy their early years of marriage much more without such a financial burden. One of the huge pleasures of bumping into that happy couple from time to time is to hear their gratitude again and again,

even today, years later! A bank's priority is more people borrowing more money. A support couple's priority is more families having better relationships. Money problems are the enemy of good relationships. Be bold!

Individual issues

Adult child of divorce

One in four children in the UK now emerges into adulthood from a single-parent home. This situation is virtually guaranteed to worsen owing to the growing trend towards out-of-wedlock births and the horrendous break-up rates of unmarried couples. Why this is so serious is that children of divorce, as a group, tend to face far higher risks of a whole range of problems – to our health, our well-being, our wealth, our behaviour and our relationships. I say "our" because I am one. While nobody is condemned to this and most kids do fine – on the outside at least – the odds are stacked against us unless we do something about it.

None of this should be very surprising. Single parents face huge pressures to rebuild their personal lives as well as to cope as parents. They have less time available to spend with their kids supervising, discussing, playing, doing fun things, helping with homework. They have less money available, which reduces choices and often brings major financial difficulties. Going to work is now more a necessity than an option. Staying at home as a full-time parent is no longer realistic. Finding a new shoulder to lean on may become hugely important. No wonder kids do less well in single-parent homes, often having to cope with the presence of another adult, or stream of adults, whose priority is the parent and not the kids. The foggy and distorted lens of children of divorce is therefore the way we view marriage and relationships.

Children of divorce need to know that we are not uniquely odd. In fact we tend to behave in fairly typical ways. It can be hugely liberating for children of divorce, and those marrying children of divorce, to become aware of this. Discovering that the way you think and behave is normal – if not always healthy – can be a huge spur to accepting each other in marriage and working out a better way ahead. Mentoring is especially helpful in this – for many people it is the first normal marriage they have witnessed at first hand. Knowing what normal marriage looks like, with its ups and downs, is especially important to the child of divorce.

But, once again, awareness of the problem is half the battle. Researcher Judith Wallerstein outlines some typical patterns of behaviour for children of divorce. The way the child handles the divorce can deeply influence the way they seek their own subsequent adult relationships.

For children, divorce is not a one-off event but a cumulative experience that peaks in early adulthood. At the point of break-up, most children are surprised. Few are relieved. Mostly, the reasons for the divorce remain a black hole. Even where there is violence, children don't link it with the decision to divorce. They may be frightened and angry, terrified of being abandoned, often feeling in some way responsible. Looking back as adults, they remember having to adjust to a confusing new world with little support from their parents. They presume thereafter that all relationships are fragile and unreliable, including their own relationship with their parents. They remember loss of an intact family and loss of their newly preoccupied parents.

Resilient children are able to draw on other resources, people or abilities. But taking responsibility for themselves, and maybe for others in their family, often comes at the cost of their own childhood. Those with less resilience view their parents and childhood with sorrow and anger. *"I never want a child of mine to experience a childhood like I had."* Teenage experiences with sex, alcohol and drugs are more common than among children from intact marriages.

But it is as adults that children of divorce tend to suffer most. For many, divorce remains the central issue of life. They lack a healthy model of love, intimacy and commitment. *"No one taught me,"* they complain. They often end up with unsuitable or troubled partners. They are anxious about their relationships. They are wary of trust and commitment. They fear disaster and loss when things are going well. They fear abandonment and rejection when things are going badly. Children of divorce struggle with differences and even moderate conflict in marriage. Their first response is often panic and then flight.

Children of divorce say things like this:

* *"What is to keep the same fate from happening to me?"*
* *"Marriage can work for others but not for me"*
* *"I fear that any marriage can just dissolve"*
* *"People think they know me, but they don't. I've learned lots of times it's better not to feel."*

So what can children of divorce do to improve their odds? They can read Judith Wallerstein's book or get a tape of one of her talks (via www.smartmarriages.com). They can become aware that their behaviour is probably quite normal, if unhealthy. They can discuss the subject with greater awareness and insight with other children of divorce, with their pastor or support couple, and with their spouse or future spouse. They can make themselves aware of their doubts and fears about relationships and how that translates into self-destructive behaviours, especially when under pressure. By doing this they will become more aware of themselves, and more accepting of themselves.

Children of divorce know that love and good marriage exist somewhere. The trick is to help them realise that, with work, it can be that way for them.

Insecurity, Depression, Substance abuse, Child abuse

One of the great benefits of being a support couple to those who are getting married is that in general both man and woman want to make their relationship work out. They are there with a positive attitude towards their marriage. This may sound obvious. But very occasionally you come across couples of whom one or the other is really unsure about whether getting married is the right thing to do. This then becomes more like dealing with couples who are having problems. Much of the time, these issues are resolved very positively through the structure of an inventory and the process of discussing all areas of their relationship.

However, where major individual problems are present, mentoring may not be enough. Insecurity and depression are illnesses of the mind that need to be treated professionally. Here are two excellent examples of situations where I would definitely suggest an individual gets some one-to-one counselling.

Both insecurity and depression are forms of thinking the worst. Insecurity involves negative self-worth. *I don't know who I am. Even if you're nice to me, I don't trust that you mean it. And anyway you won't be there tomorrow.* In some ways it's the opposite of commitment. Insecurity might make me very vulnerable to social influence. If somebody says get married, I get married. Or it might make me fearful and isolated. *Nobody cares so it's best not to venture out of my shell and risk getting hurt.* Or it might make me wear a social mask, such as wonderful socialite or good person or perfectionist. That's fine until I need to reveal my true self in my most intimate relationship: marriage.

The only way through insecurity is to talk it all out until it suddenly clicks that I am accepted for who I am. That can be done perfectly well with close friends. However, the chances are that the insecure have few close friends in the first place because insecurity does not make people especially attractive. The best course of action is to send them off to a one-to-one counsellor, for whom this is bread-and-butter stuff.

Depression involves negative automatic thoughts, usually triggered by some life event, leading to a sense of hopelessness, doom, gloom and feeling trapped. Life feels like being in a black room or a tunnel with no way out. I'm stranded in the middle of the ocean with no possibility of rescue. I give up. My situation is hopeless. Whatever I do is pointless. Suicide may be an option. The three most common treatments for this are antidepressant medication, cognitive behavioural therapy and reflective counselling.

The current consensus is that a mixture of talk and tablets is the best way to deal with depression. Whether negative automatic thoughts cause the neurones in the brain to change their function, or the other way round, is not very clear. But a reasonable premise is that negative thought processes lead to chemical imbalance which in turn makes thought processes more negative. Antidepressant tablets are supposed to reverse the chemical imbalance more or less immediately and thereby allow the brain to think more clearly. During that time, you hope that therapy or counselling encourages the development of less negative and more positive thought processes, which then prevent the chemical imbalance from recurring. The best course of action here is to send them to a GP, who may well prescribe antidepressants and refer their patient for counselling.

I've only once come across a problem with drugs or alcohol. Undoubtedly it exists in an ever greater number of people. But as my experience is seriously limited in this area, I almost always suggest they talk to their GP or another professional agency with whom they may already have had contact. Trying to help make a marriage work when drugs or alcohol are messing up someone's mind is like rearranging the deckchairs on the *Titanic*. A waste of time.

Finally, child abuse. If the subject comes up, there is no need to take a sharp intake of breath and run away. Support couples can help tremendously just by being there. Most of the time, child abuse will be something the couple need to discuss at length, in detail, privately, and over time. It may also be something that needs to be dealt with at an individual level with a one-to-one counsellor. Unless the couple explicitly request it, this should not be support-couple territory directly. However, it surely makes huge sense that a couple who are getting married will be far better equipped to discuss these and any other intensely difficult issues because of what they have already been able to discuss constructively in front of their support couple. With a positive attitude to one another, and with excellent communication skills, any issue can be discussed. It may be that this particular issue can be discussed with a support couple discreetly and sensitively coaching them. This would merely mean making sure they use the skills correctly. In most cases, however, I would encourage the couple to make sure they discuss it privately. A spouse who can love, accept and stay with their other half as they thrash their way through some appalling childhood memory is the kind of spouse worth having.

Summary

So there you go. I've told you all I know about dealing with difficult issues. I really don't know very much more than what I've just written. If you're a professional reading this, you probably think I haven't got much of a clue. And you're right. I haven't.

What I *do* know is what a support couple are and aren't. A support couple are a well-informed uncle and aunt. A support couple are not experts. So I really don't need to know that much about difficult issues to be one of a good enough support couple. I just need to know that I'm not the one expected to work everything out. I also need to know when to stop and where to point people.

I've divided difficult issues into three. First off are rows or arguments. This is an area where I really do know my stuff. I've had a few arguments myself and I know some highly effective ways to help couples sort things out. I don't need years of expert training to do this really well. I just have a little knowledge, a little confidence, and the will to take charge. I described the practical skills needed in Chapters 3, 4 and 5. If you recognise the bad habits, coach the good habits and know how to apply the party tricks, you're on your way to becoming an excellent support couple.

Second are issues affecting the couple. I'm starting to become a little more wary here. I know a bit about sex – having had a few kids and read some books. I've read a bit of research on cohabitation and I've thought through how to approach the subject. I know quite a bit about money – although this relates more to getting the principles right than to understanding the incomprehensible technical jargon I read in the papers on Sunday. So I'm quite happy to venture into these topics. But, equally, I'll back off if I reach my limits. Much the same will apply to you.

Third are issues affecting the individual. I'm definitely getting into deeper water here. Although I used to be qualified as a counsellor, I've untrained myself in order to be a more directive mentor. So I generally prefer to leave issues of insecurity, depression, substance abuse or child abuse to others. These are problems that take time to sort out and invariably require specialised skills. So this is where I recommend a visit to a GP or a one-to-one counsellor. Once again, the same is likely to apply to you.

The trick in all this is knowing my limits. I know what I know and what I *don't* know. I'm not embarrassed about saying *"I don't know"* or referring onwards. Every support couple will have areas of strength and weakness. You might be the opposite to me. You might be a trained counsellor who is brilliant with insecurity. Then use your talents appropriately. You might not have a clue about money. Then refer on to someone who does have a clue.

We don't have to know everything. And that is the very simple reason why I eagerly resist the professionalisation of mentoring – loads of rules, loads of supervision, loads of training. It's almost all unnecessary.

As support couples, we are not experts. We are married, which qualifies us to be uncle and aunt figures, since anyone can do that. We know a few marital tricks and skills that make us well informed. But we also know our limitations and where to stop.

References

- Heimdal, K.R. and Houseknecht, S.K. (2003) Cohabiting and married couples' income organization: Approaches in Sweden and the United States. *Journal of Marriage and Family* 65, 525–538.

Chapter 9

The proof of the pudding

In this chapter

- What couples and support couples say about mentoring
- What our evaluators tell us about mentoring courses

What people get from mentoring

The proof of the pudding is in the eating. It's all very well me banging on about what I think is important or what the research says about mentoring. What really matters is whether people enjoy the experience and benefit from it.

Here are some quotes from couples who have been mentored and some from support couples themselves. The majority of these couples have been through the programme I run in Bristol. This is a combination of a three-hour adapted version of the PREP course followed by three to six evenings with a support couple using FOCCUS. This book covers far more ground but the basic principles are much the same. To take the wider view, I've also included a brief evaluation of a sample of UK marriage preparation and mentoring programmes, three-quarters of which are outside Bristol.

What couples actually say

Chris and Alice, newly-wed, heard about course through church

"We have been really blessed by this whole process"

Chris and I attended your marriage training day in February, a month into our engagement. We were then connected up with our support couple, Simon and Shirley. We met up with them and went through the issues arising from the training day over a number of meals during the next few months. We got married in August and are planning to continue meeting up with our support couple concerning any new issues that arise.

In the light of this fantastic input into our lives as a couple, we wanted to thank you for the training day and all the follow-up work which happens so naturally through meeting up with our support couple. We have been really blessed by this whole process and thoroughly commend the skills training and mentoring work you do to help build up solid marriages.

Nick and Sophie, newly-wed, heard about course from a friend

"It comes as a great reassurance to learn that couples who have been married for some time still don't know all the answers"

We took the course just a few weeks before our wedding in June. We have been singing its praises ever since – and know of at least two couples who are going to do the course as a result.

Sophie heard about the course through a friend. I (Nick) have to say that I was very reluctant to even consider going along. My gut feeling was that it would involve cringing at Oprah-style revelations. But I went. Not only was it surprisingly painless, but some of the common-sense teaching really helped us both to identify different types of behaviour and to vent feelings that had previously been stored up over time to our detriment.

Our support couple, Claire and Ian, were great. Any apprehensions about awkwardness were swept away as soon as we arrived at their house. They guided us swiftly through the material we had to cover, with plenty of laughs along the way. Some of the more serious subjects were made much easier to tackle when Claire and Ian offered some of their own experiences and expressed some of the difficulties they had encountered. It comes as a great reassurance to learn that couples who have been married for some time still don't know all the answers.

I suppose the one thing I've taken away from the meetings is the knowledge that it's fine to have differences – even big ones. But there are three vital keys to a happy relationship: communication, having an awareness of negative behaviour, and having the tools to avoid or deal with it.

The course is invaluable.

Carl and Jayme, newly-wed, heard about course through church

"It wasn't until we took the course that we realised that there was so much more we hadn't talked about"

We had heard that communication was vitally important to any successful relationship and we thought we had it figured out. We met in Japan and began to correspond after Carl had gone back to the UK. I (Jayme) still had three months left on my teaching contract, after which I would be going home to Canada. There were long periods of time when we weren't able to see each other, so we spoke on the phone, used e-mail, post and the Internet a great deal.

As a result of this, we knew our relationship was very strong, especially in terms of communication. When I finally moved to the UK we kept on communicating and talking things through (this time in person!), but it wasn't until we took the course that we realised that there was so much more we hadn't talked about. A lot of things surfaced that we hadn't even thought to discuss. Armed with our speaker/listener skills, we set about communicating properly.

We are aware of things like Thinking the Worst and Opting Out and we now recognise it and can put a name to it. We are still not perfect, but we feel very confident that there is nothing that we cannot talk through and resolve. Indeed, none of our infrequent arguments has lasted more than a few hours. We feel closer than ever now and would recommend this course to anyone!

We are now married and are feeling very confident that ours is a love that will last.

Matt and Claire, newly-wed, heard about course through church

"We have found that this course has given us more confidence"

We found the mentoring useful on lots of different levels. We learned lessons from our support couple on both what to do and what not to do! We think that the most valuable issues we worked through were the practical but life-shaping ones –

who was going to take a lead with the finances, if we had kids who would stay at home, what we felt about family involvement, the compatibility of our beliefs. We knew the answers before we tied the knot and were happy with them. Obviously, circumstances can change, and some of those things might change, but we feel that we had a really solid foundation to start with.

We are both fortunate to come from backgrounds where both sets of parents are still happily married to their original partners and so felt confident about marriage. But we have found that this course has given us more confidence. We felt like we had exhausted a huge list of issues and, though they may have provided some lively debate, the fact that we have clarity on them gives us reassurance now.

The mentoring also gave us focus in the run-up to the wedding, a time that can be chaotic and stressful. It helped us to focus on the 50 years after the wedding – the marriage – rather than on what colour the napkins should be or whether sugared almonds were really a necessity. We even became friends with our support couple and had great fun getting to know both them and their children.

Ian and Sarah, newly-wed, heard about course through church

"Looking back now it seems strange that we had not thought it the most natural thing in the world to speak to a married couple of several years' standing about the reality of marriage"

"Would you like to go on a marriage preparation course?" was not quite the proposal I had been hoping for in the run up to the second anniversary of dating Ian. I had been hoping for champagne, flowers and a ring a lot sooner. However,

I knew that it would be a means for us to see whether an honest look at ourselves and our relationship would give us confidence enough to get married or the courage to split up.

As the evenings with our mentoring couple progressed, I found that it was a safe environment in which I could express fears and doubts. The gentle guidance of our support couple directed our conversations to ensure that we took on board and thought about what our partner was saying. The environment of mentoring helped us to talk and to listen. We came to see that sometimes in the past our discussions on important areas had fallen into a pattern of each making room for the other to talk before we could carry on with what we wanted to say. Sometimes perhaps we were not actually processing what the other was saying and feeling.

The input from the support couple was fairly minimal. It soon became obvious that they were not there to take sides in our arguments/discussions or even to say whether they thought we were right or wrong. They did share with us their own experiences where it was relevant to what we were going through. For example, how they coped with different attitudes to spending, to different ways of relaxing and to big questions such as deciding when to have children or where to live. Their input was never intended (or taken) as a formula to be followed.

Now that we are married, some of the things that I frequently recall our support couple saying relate to negative things that they shared; not negative things about each other, but being real about struggles that they have faced. They added an element of reality at a time when romanticism could easily have taken over and soon faded to leave a couple disillusioned with the vague feeling that they were sure they must have been tricked into something somewhere along the line as marital bliss had not pervaded their every waking moment from honeymoon onwards.

Looking back now it seems strange that we had not thought it the most natural thing in the world to speak to a married couple of several years' standing about the reality of marriage. While having fun dating we did not have at the forefront of our minds the fact that marriage would be for life. Now that we have truly discovered that, we can see how worthwhile it was to check out what it all means in practical terms with someone who knows.

Andy and Donna, newly-wed, heard about course at a wedding fair

"I think what we drew out of the sessions were very much the positives rather than the negatives about our relationship"

We participated in your course about March and had five or six mentoring sessions with Tanya and Daniel before getting married in July. I hit it off straight away with Tanya on the phone, as she is from Australia and we are relocating to Australia in the new year for a couple of years. So straight away I sensed that this mentoring experience was not going to be too traumatic. I don't know if Donna was totally convinced; this was in part because we sensed (rightly or wrongly) that the whole concept of pre-marriage consulting has religious undertones – whatever. We are not religious.

As it happened, though, Tanya and Daniel were a very friendly and fun couple and we enjoyed the sessions very much. I think what we drew out of the sessions were very much the positives rather than the negatives about our relationship. Fortunately, we don't have to deal with a lot of the issues that can be problematic for other couples, e.g. families, different ethnic backgrounds, money problems, etc. We had been together for 8 1/2 years so we didn't really touch on any new ground, as it were. The mentoring forum did allow us to raise a few things that wouldn't have been talked about otherwise. These weren't major things, though, really.

To friends getting married we would talk about our experiences; we would tell them we found it beneficial and we would suggest that they try it. For them to actually do it is their decision. I hope that the message is getting through. Keep up the good work.

I don't know if I can attribute it to the mentoring, but we have been getting on as well as ever over the last few months!

Al and Fi, newly-wed, heard about the course through church

"Our support couple encouraged us when we said we're not jealous people. Other people may not have that"

We were going through a bit of a wobble in our relationship and went to a couple for some advice. They suggested we do the support-couple course. Our first reaction was surprise because we weren't yet engaged. But we were reassured that it was OK.

The questionnaire was really interesting. Lots of questions about things way ahead in the future that I'd never really thought about, e.g. children. I enjoyed the questionnaire and I enjoyed the mentoring. I loved those evenings. I really enjoyed discussing things with two other people. It made it so much less heated. The course made us think about how to bring our different views together. It really pushed through some obstacles. Previously, for example, I used to be told things in a way that felt like nagging, and it made me angry. The course helped us find a better way.

Just discussing things out loud was encouraging. Like

when our support couple encouraged us when we said we're not jealous people. Other people may not have that. I came away thinking, yes, there's no major problems and lots of positive things. We would probably have got engaged anyway but it was really reassuring.

What support couples say

Trevor and Sue, support couple, married 30 years, mentored two couples

"As a support couple, we have found this a valuable experience"

We have been going through questions and situations with couples, which would have been really useful to have discussed at the onset of our own marriage. Thirty years on we have a wealth of experience under our belts, but mostly gained through 'interesting' times. Maybe we would still have gone through them even if we'd done an inventory at the time. But we both agree that couples can only benefit from marriage mentoring as they talk through the many situations that may come their way.

Helen and Simon, support couple, married 17 years, mentored four couples

"We really enjoy getting to know the couples, but I have to be on my guard against a tendency to want to solve everyone's problems for them"

We were pretty nervous when we started, even though the support-couple training had been helpful and practical. But I

(Helen) felt convinced it was a way of putting our own experience of marriage (extremely happy but having coped with depression and hepatitis C, having twins and multiple family bereavements) to good use. Funnily enough, although I was the more keen to start with, after our first (very positive) experience Simon is now happy to take the lead! We feel that the mentoring process is really valuable for all couples, and it has helped us to be honest with each other about some aspects of our relationship that we don't often discuss and has made us value our own marriage even more.

We really enjoy getting to know the couples, but I have to be on my guard against a tendency to want to solve everyone's problems for them, because the aim is for them to learn to do it themselves! I would recommend mentoring to any couple who are concerned about family breakdown and feel they can share their experiences openly with new people.

Rob and Lynden, support couple

"We both grew in confidence"

At first the materials seemed daunting; however, after the first two sessions we were at ease and found we were working really well as a team.

I started to notice how good Rob was at putting the engaged couple at their ease and also his unerring "nose" for the underlying issues.

He noticed that I was good at preparing the sessions and managing them. We both grew in confidence, especially about interrupting each other if we saw an important issue to address, or needed to refocus the couple towards each other rather than talking to us.

Silas and Annie, support couple, married 16 years, mentored one couple

"I didn't know I felt trained until I started doing it"

After only one day of training, I didn't know I felt trained until I started doing it. We've met our couple twice so far and it's going really well.

Marilyn and Derek, support couple, married 41 years, mentored seven couples

"It has been a privilege to be alongside couples and see their relationships develop and grow"

We fell into mentoring quite unexpectedly through hosting an overseas couple who were visiting our church to talk about mentoring. As reasonable hosts we transported them to the meetings, and found ourselves taking part in the training day because of their encouragement! We decided our only qualification for mentoring was that after 40+ years we have made enough mistakes to share our experiences with others just starting out on marriage!

Because our vicar asked us to mentor a couple at very short notice, we had to work out how to use FOCCUS on our own in just a few hours. In retrospect it was a good start to our mentoring, as we learned how valuable the material was and how it could be used very flexibly. Even after such a hurried start, we had a lovely letter from the couple thanking us and noting how valuable our few hours together had been.

Subsequently we have mentored six couples referred through our church and our local CFT, using a fuller programme of skills training followed by mentoring. We found we could adapt the programme for specific needs. One initially very reluctant partner told us how much they'd enjoyed the experience and recognised it as valuable for their relationship.

We've found mentoring good for our own marriage. Even in a training session we found ourselves sharing something we had each held on to for several years. Talking it through helped us to move on to understand why and how our different perceptions of that experience had been so painful at the time.

It has been a privilege to be alongside couples and see their relationships develop and grow during the period of the programme; to feel some of the pain as couples have opened up about early life experiences that they are carrying into their marriage relationships; to breathe a sigh of relief as couples have eventually felt able to trust each other with doubts and anxieties that they had previously not been able to talk about. And now, after the big day has passed, to watch couples growing closer, enjoying and encouraging each other in their life together.

A by-product has been the pleasure of sharing in so many wedding celebrations. Our own son and daughter joke about us being professional wedding guests, and have taken to enquiring if we are available at weekends, or are we attending yet another wedding!

Simon and Shirley, support couple, married 4 1/2 years, mentored one couple

"Now that we've had a go we would love to do another couple next year"

Being a support couple has been a fantastic experience and we've really loved it. That's partly due to the fact we had probably the most sorted couple in the world, but also because the material is very good. We met Chris and Alice about four times before they got married. We did know them a little before we started the mentoring process, but had such a good time that they asked Simon to do the address at their wedding.

We have had a lot of issues to work out in our marriage, and being a support couple has given us not only more tools to tackle our stuff with, but also a regular opportunity to think about our relationship where we might not otherwise make the time. For example, we were discussing with our couple the significance of communicating rather than agreeing as they began to recognise some areas of difference between them. Later that week we had a disagreement. We ended up reminding each other of what we'd said to our couple and chose to communicate instead of sulk!

I think we both felt nervous to start with – it's just human nature and probably all support couples feel it – but we found the inventory was very easy to use. Now that we've had a go we would love to do another couple next year. We have found we are using ideas and skills from the training in our own marriage and the subject of mentoring often comes up when talking to friends.

We received a letter from our couple, bits of which I can pass on. I feel funny writing this because it's very flattering, but I think it's good for you to know how well it worked for them:

> *I wanted to say thank you so much to you and Simon for your "mentoring" of us. We have really enjoyed the conversation, appreciated the wisdom and insight regarding our relationship and each other and feel really affirmed as a couple re all these things. Thank you for asking, listening, advising and*

praying! Most of all, though, Chris and I have loved being able to hang out with you both and your kids and simply being able to get to know you and enjoy meals with you! Thanks for being friends to us as well as a support couple!

Mike and Nathalie, support couple, married 11 years, mentored one couple

"I learned that I can actually listen and not talk. Mike learned that he can talk and not just listen"

Our first experience of mentoring has been very positive, resulting in being invited to Carl and Jayme's wedding and reception. That was wonderful. One very good thing about mentoring is that it does tend to establish a friendship quickly! We look forward to mentoring our second couple.

Before the first session we did have the wobbles – perfect strangers over for a meal: help! But doing a meal and having a drink really helps things along. Also, the couple are committed to doing the course, so it is OK! We covered all the subjects in about six sessions. We basically spent a bit more time on items the couple knew were a problem – where they had disagreed and wanted to discuss where they stood now. We spent a bit less time on things they really felt they had discussed, or they had no problems with. Over mealtimes we shared some of our own experiences, which they asked about, so it did not encroach on their "talking time".

It has been really good for us to do something as important and positive as marriage mentoring. Mike and I are even more convinced of the importance of good communication now. We have been so blessed in so many ways by others as regards communication. It is good to give back.

Tim and Julie, support couple, married 10 years, mentored one couple

"For us it was good to think about the questions ourselves and to feel that we've come a long way since we got married"

We thought our one-day support-couple training course did a good job in preparing us for the first time. It gives you enough to feel that you have a rough framework to work with without being overly prescriptive. We *loved* the dance!

We enjoyed mentoring. It was a great opportunity to get to know a couple whom we didn't know that well, and hopefully for them to get to know us. For us it was good to think about the questions ourselves and to feel that we've come a long way since we got married.

We hope our couple benefited from the mentoring! We did three sessions with our couple. Lifestyle Expectations and Communication both took a session each and were probably the most useful sessions. It gave them confidence that they have talked through so much prior to getting married as well as providing a focused time to talk together about things that came up in the weeks before we met up.

Formal evaluation of mentoring

The first formal evaluation of UK marriage preparation – using mentoring and inventories – took place in late 2003. Academics from Exeter University analysed 733 response forms from ten Community Family Trusts (CFTs) around the UK – including the project I run in Bristol. 343 forms were completed before a course and 390 forms afterwards.

Participants tended to be better-educated, higher-income, church-going couples. 54% had university-level education;

82% of participants earned income above the national average, and 56% were regular churchgoers. In some areas of life, the sample was more representative. For example, 68% of couples were cohabiting and 29% came from broken homes.

All the CFTs were using inventories. Nearly all used the FOCCUS inventory and nearly all used support couple rather than single facilitators.

The evaluation showed that mentoring increases confidence well above already high starting levels, across a range of ten issues relevant to married life. Levels of confidence increased especially in being able to discuss *"sharing hopes and dreams"*, *"sexual behaviour"* and *"making decisions"*. Programmes also had a particular impact on areas where people feel most doubtful to begin with, notably *"resolving conflict"*, *"sexual behaviour"* and *"issues about finance"*.

Among issues overall, 85% of couples said they were confident before the course started, 92% of couples said they were

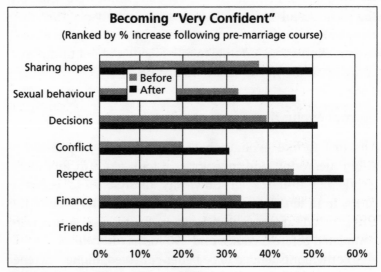

Becoming "Very Confident"
(Ranked by % increase following pre-marriage course)

Figure 9.1 Course evaluation (1)

Figure 9.2 Course evaluation (2)

confident afterwards. The percentage of couples who said they were *"very confident"* rose from 36% beforehand to 47% afterwards. Given such very high levels of confidence to begin with, it is remarkable that positive change can be recorded at all.

On seven of ten issues surveyed, improvements in confidence were both substantial and "statistically significant", i.e. not likely to be due to mere chance.

Satisfaction with CFT marriage-preparation programmes was also very high and few were dissatisfied. Fewer than 10% of people found their course either boring, unsupportive, uninformative or embarrassing. Just 2% did not enjoy their course and only one person found it other than well organised. Well over 90% of people said they found their course well organised, enjoyable, informative, supportive, not scary, not embarrassing, neither boring nor dull, and would recommend it to friends.

People said the courses especially made a difference with

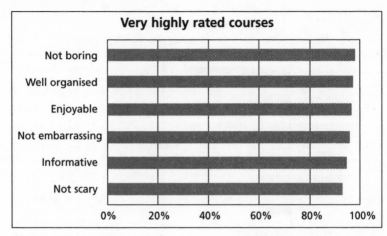

Figure 9.3 Course ratings

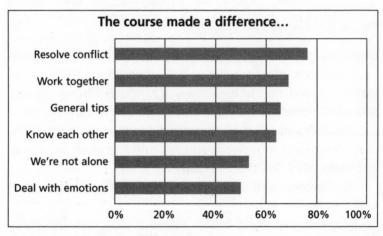

Figure 9.4 Making a difference

"resolving conflict" (76%), "working together" (69%), "general tips" (68%), "knowing each other better" (65%), "knowing we're not alone" (53%) and "dealing with emotions" (50%).

Summary

I hope that's a pretty encouraging summary of what people actually say about mentoring. Mentoring is much appreciated, not only by couples getting married but also by the support couples themselves. Of the 80-odd couples I have trained as support couples in Bristol and elsewhere so far, I know of only two couples who have formally given up after just one go at mentoring.

Couples talk about mentoring as a positive experience that leaves them confident and reassured – not least that it's OK to have differences.

Support couples talk about mentoring as a privilege as well as a valuable experience for their own marriage.

And it's not just that I've selected some juicy quotes from those who have taken the trouble to write their thoughts down. Formal independent evaluation says that this positive experience is almost universal. On average, engaged or newly-wed couples finish mentoring with significantly greater confidence about their marriage, especially regarding areas where there is most concern. Over 90% of those being mentored found lots of positive things and no negative things to say about their mentoring experience.

Undoubtedly, mentoring isn't everybody's cup of tea. Fewer than 5% of those surveyed clearly didn't enjoy themselves much. I don't know whether that's because of them or their support couple or their expectations, or whatever. It still seems like a remarkably small percentage compared to other courses I've come across.

Despite these outstanding testimonies, mentoring remains an unfamiliar idea, especially in the UK. At the moment, very few people are being mentored before they get married. The overwhelming majority of those having civil weddings are neither offered nor aware of any kind of marriage education whatsoever.

A government-sponsored survey carried out on behalf of the Church of England in Guildford suggested that only about 20% of couples getting married in church have any serious marriage preparation at all, as opposed to wedding preparation. That means even the church is probably only covering about 5% of the entire wedding market. CFTs are starting to make slow progress in promoting the concept. In our second year at Bristol CFT, for example, we trained around 70 of the 1,800 couples getting married in Bristol. That's a start, but it's still only a tiny minority of couples.

But we have hope. In both the US and Australia, where marriage education is better established, access to marriage preparation using inventories has now reached 15–20% nationally. It is most likely that a further 15–20% of couples do some other form of marriage preparation. However because these are averages, take-up in some areas can be as high as 100%.

We may not have exactly the same culture as the Americans or the Australians, but there are undoubted similarities. If they can do it there, we can do it as well. In the UK, exciting new ventures that actively involve the civil registrars, responsible for two-thirds of weddings, look likely to give us greater access to couples than ever before.

The proof of the pudding is that people really enjoy mentoring and being mentored. More good stories and better access to couples give us a serious opportunity to begin turning back the appalling and unnecessary tide of marriage breakdown – from the bottom up.

Part Two

Chapter 10   **The case for marriage**

In this chapter

- Research shows that marriage is generally good
- Research shows that cohabitation is generally not good
- Research shows that divorce is generally bad

Note

There are striking similarities among the anglophone countries when it comes to high divorce, cohabitation and unmarried birth rates. Because I know the UK best, I've reviewed the state of UK marriage as an example of this before moving on to more general research findings on marital status. There are differences between countries, of course. For example, divorce rates in the US are higher than in the UK but are showing signs of falling. If you need information for the US or other countries, may I refer you to www.smartmarriages.com. All data except where stated is sourced from the Office of National Statistics.

The decline of marriage

Marriage is in decline, according to the 2001 UK census. The proportion of all UK households containing a married couple had fallen from 64% in 1981 to 55% in 1991 and 45% in 2001. Some commentators suggest that, at this rate of decline, married households are heading for extinction by 2050. In reality, of course, this won't happen. Even if the current down-trend continues, extinction is well over 100 years away. A lot

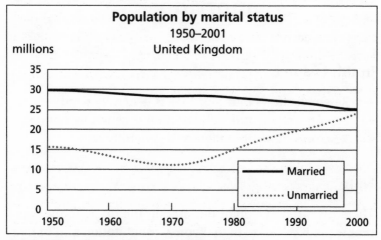

Figure 10.1 Population by marital status

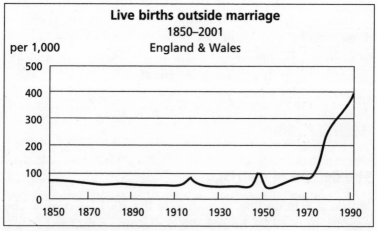

Figure 10.2 Births outside marriage

can happen in that time! Marriage may be on its way down. But it is a very long way from being out.

Nonetheless, as far as marriage is concerned, the public is voting with its feet. Marriage is now viewed as just one of several possible lifestyle choices. What is most important, people are saying, is that children are brought up in a stable, loving home. But we don't need the census to tell us that marriage is in decline. Since the 1960s, the proportion of babies born to unmarried parents has increased from 5% to 40%. The old label of "illegitimate" now seems strangely irrelevant to those many parents who are unmarried.

UK marriage and divorce

After rising steadily from the war, the number of new marriages began to decline from 1970. Marriage *rates* have now fallen even more sharply than marriage *numbers*. While there are half as many new marriages today compared to 1970, the marriage rate is just one quarter of what it was. The huge increase in divorces in the 1970s has led the next generation to turn their backs on marriage. Who could blame them? Marriage didn't work for their parents. They want something better and getting married doesn't seem to be it.

To emphasise the importance of this link, there is a startling correlation between the number of births outside marriage and the number of divorces 16 years earlier. Figure 10.4 shows the amazing overlap. It's almost a perfect match.

From the war until the mid-1960s, the number of divorces also rose from virtually zero to around 25,000 per year. The divorce rate in the 1950s and 1960s was just 0.2% per year. In 1969, family law changed, allowing "no fault" divorces after two years had elapsed. Numbers of divorces soared to around 160,000 per year. The annual divorce rate soared to 0.8% in

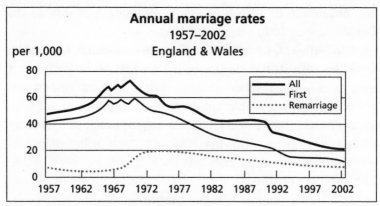

Figure 10.3 Annual marriage rates

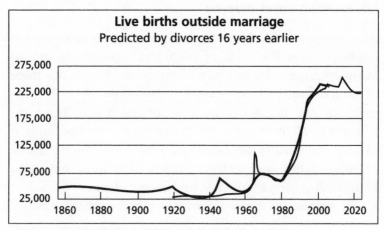

Figure 10.4 Divorces and births outside marriage

1970 and 1.2% in 1980. Thereafter, divorce rates have remained consistently around 1.3% per year.

Nor do people seem to learn from their mistakes. I estimate that about 1.2% of first marriages fail every year, compared to about 2.1% of second marriages. Second marriages in the UK are therefore about 80% more likely to fail than first marriages.

Most people want to know what this means for the over-

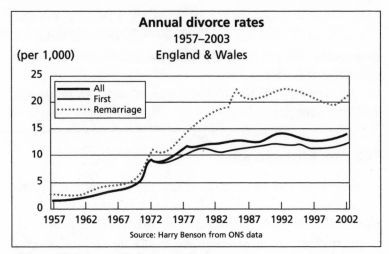

Figure 10.5 Annual divorce rates

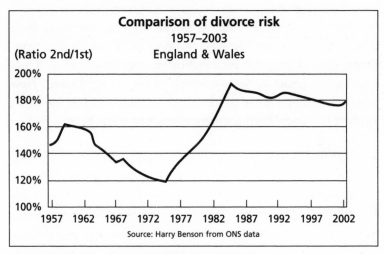

Figure 10.6 Comparison of divorce risk

all divorce rate. The only reliable way to find out divorce rates is to follow groups of people who got married in a particular year and see how many of them get divorced over time. This allows us to make an informed guess as to how many of today's new marriages will fail. In the UK, I estimate the lifetime risk of divorce for a couple getting married today at about 45%. The risk for first marriages is 35% and for second marriages it is 65%.

So, despite what we read in the press, most UK marriages still last a lifetime.

The case for marriage

Of course the rise in divorces is not the only reason for the reduction in new marriages. It is also a symptom of a wider trend. Perhaps the major underlying driving force is our cultural emphasis on *my* freedom, *my* rights, *my* comfort and *my* happiness as a consumer. If I'm not happy with my marriage, then I get a new one.

In following our instincts for personal satisfaction, freedom and rights, we have gone very badly astray. Far from being one of many lifestyle choices, marriage remains the best family structure within which to bring up children. New research findings since the 1990s confirm that what the great faiths have been saying for thousands of years is true.

- Getting married is generally a good idea
- Living together without getting married is generally not a good idea
- Getting divorced or splitting up is generally a bad idea.

Why getting married is a good idea

Across the world, an array of studies show comprehensively that, compared to the unmarried, married people tend to be happier and healthier, to live longer, earn more, work harder, and save more. According to Linda Waite and Maggie

Gallagher (2000) in their book *The Case for Marriage*, the many benefits and protections attributed to marriage are largely due to the attitudes and behaviours resulting from commitment.

Firstly, the long-term nature of commitment allows each spouse to risk either specialising or letting go of certain domestic roles – such as responsibility for children's clothes, family accounts, food-planning, wage-earning. Specialisation is a more efficient arrangement than equal sharing in terms of time, stress and money.

Secondly, commitment motivates a couple to look out for each other. These two factors account for much of the reason why married people appear healthier and wealthier than the unmarried. A third reason is that married couples also tend to receive more social and financial support from both extended families.

An obvious complaint against these supposed benefits of marriage is that married people are only happier, healthier and wealthier simply because they started off that way in the first place. This is what social scientists call a "selection effect". This claim has now been shown to be only partly true at best, and often quite false.

Take depression, for example. Men marry or not regardless of whether they are depressed. Yet those who marry become less depressed and those who then divorce become more depressed. Take physical health as another example. Married people are healthier. Yet unhealthy people actually marry at a younger age than their healthy counterparts.

The reality is that getting and staying married reflects beneficial changes in attitude and behaviour that undoubtedly cause these accompanying benefits and protections. Without making things too complicated, let's look at a few of these studies.

Marriage, happiness and well-being

In spite of the bad press marriage often receives, married people as a group are far more likely to be happy and far less likely to be unhappy than any other group of people. A ten-year survey of 14,000 adults found that marital status was one of the most important predictors of happiness (Davis, 1984). A later analysis of this sample found that 40% of the married said they were "happy" with life, compared to only 15–22% of any of the non-married groups – whether separated, divorced, cohabitees, widows, or singles. Likewise, only 7% of the married said they were "not too happy", compared to 13–27% of other non-married groups (Waite and Gallagher, 2000). Two long-term studies have specifically ruled out the possibility that married people simply start out happier and better adjusted. One study found that mental health improved consistently and substantially upon getting married and deteriorated substantially upon getting divorced or separated (Marks & Lambert, 1998). Another found that the lower rates of alcoholism in married women and depression in married men could not be due to selection (Horwitz et al., 1996).

Marriage, health and mortality

Married people are less likely to suffer from long-term illnesses (Murphy et al., 1997) and far less likely to die in hospital as surgical patients (Goodwin et al., 1987). Marriage apparently helps us live longer. One typical long-term study looked at 6,000 families and took all sorts of factors into account, such as race, education, location, children and income. This study found that a 48-year-old woman was more than twice as likely to die in any given year before reaching age 65 if she was divorced rather than married (18%

vs 8%). Divorced men were three times more likely to die during this period (35% vs 12%). This finding was particularly interesting because it showed that the big difference was not between those who lived alone and those who didn't but between the married and the unmarried (Lillard & Waite, 1995).

It has long been argued from household surveys that men do especially well out of marriage, because single men are more likely to engage in risky behaviour such as smoking or drinking. However, a recent study of British census data, which includes people in hospital or care homes, shows that both unmarried men *and* women occupy a hugely disproportionate share of institutional beds compared to their share of the population. Both men's and women's health and longevity benefit from marriage (Hayes & Prior, 2003).

Marriage, wealth and poverty

Marriage not only makes people work harder and save more, it also makes them less likely to get into poverty. *"One of the most well-documented phenomena in social science"*, according to Waite and Gallagher (2000), is the 10–40% wage premium earned by married men compared to the unmarried. This phenomenon is common to almost all developed countries (Schoeni, 1995). The wage premium emerges in the year before marriage, increases during marriage, and erodes with divorce, even after taking other factors into account (Daniel, 1995). In effect, these higher salaries reflect the greater productivity of married workers. In the US, for example, the average 30% wage premium is equivalent to the extra salary gained from having a university degree!

Not only do married people earn more, they also save more. One study found that US married couples in their 50s and 60s had a net worth per person roughly double that of divorcees, widows or other unmarried people. Over a five-year period, married people saved faster, even accounting for education and health. Higher earnings accounted for less than a third of the disparity in wealth (Smith, 1995).

Other studies looking at the other end of the economic scale find that marriage appears to protect people from poverty. For example, among US families without high-school education (the equivalent of UK A-levels), 40% of single mothers were poor compared to 12% of married mothers. Among those with high-school education, 12% of single mothers were poor compared to 3% of married mothers (McLanahan & Sandefur, 1994).

Why living together without getting married is generally not a good idea

In the UK, an estimated 70–90% of couples who marry have also cohabited beforehand. Received wisdom is that living together before marriage is a good way to test a relationship. Many have concluded that there is no longer any need or point in marrying at all. Yet the evidence is very compelling in suggesting that precisely the opposite is true.

Unmarried couples and break-up rates

We hear endlessly about the importance of *"committed stable couples in long-term relationships"*. Yet outside marriage, such couples are few and far between. Many studies have demonstrated the relative instability of unmarried couples. Just one tenth of unmarried couples are still together happily unmarried ten years later. The rest have either married or split up (Ermisch & Francesconi, 1998).

Unmarried couples in the UK are four to five times more likely to break up in any given period than married couples are (Boheim & Ermisch, 1999; Lindgren, 1997). This may seem obvious before a couple has children. Yet sadly it remains true even after children are born. A study by Kathleen Kiernan (1999) of the London School of Economics found that whether you are a baby born to married or unmarried parents makes a huge difference to your odds of having both parents around throughout your childhood. 43% of unmarried parents will have split up before their child's fifth birthday, compared to 8% of married parents.

Many studies across the world also find that living together before marriage raises the risk of subsequent divorce by around 40–85%. This is especially true of multiple cohabitees (Bumpass & Sweet, 1995; Kahn & London, 1991; Haskey, 1992). Interestingly, some studies, though not all, have found that living together while engaged had no effect on the subsequent marriage (Teachman, 2003). This seems to suggest

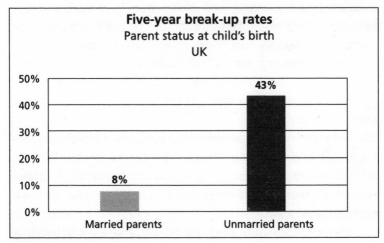

Figure 10.7 Five-year break-up rates

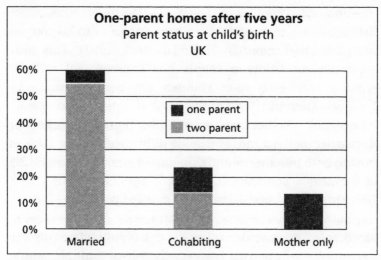

Figure 10.8 One-parent homes after five years

that engaged couples who live together behave as if they are already married, and differently from those who live together without marriage plans.

One objection to these findings is that couples who cohabited in the 1960s and 1970s were a minority group. Perhaps it was not cohabitation that was the problem but some other factors that also make people more likely to cohabit. Yet the big gap in both marital quality and divorce rates between those who cohabit before marriage and those who don't remains the same in the 1980s and 1990s (Kamp Dush *et al.*, 2003).

A major study of several thousand low-income families for the UK Department of Work and Pensions (Marsh & Perry, 2003) showed that cohabitation is a risk factor for relationship breakdown, regardless of people's earnings, age, income, employment or race.

These studies, and others like them, make it crystal clear that cohabitation itself reduces the odds of a successful relationship. Marriage keeps parents together, not children. The break-up of unmarried families – not divorce – is now responsible for rising family breakdown.

Unmarried couples and personal safety

Contrary to the impression given by the media, marriage actually protects against the risks of child abuse or domestic violence. Being unmarried appears to make an especially big difference to these risks. One UK study found that rates of serious abuse among children living with both unmarried biological parents were an astonishing 20 times higher than for children living with both married biological parents. The additional risk was also six times higher in stepfamilies, 14–20 times higher with a single parent, and 33 times higher with mother and live-in boyfriend (Whelan, 1994). Studies in the US confirm the vastly increased risk of abuse from a live-in non-parent (Daly & Wilson, 1998). Occurrences of domestic violence are also several times higher among unmarried partners, even when education, race, age and gender are taken into account (Waite and Gallagher, 2000).

So, while being married protects against abuse and domestic violence, being unmarried raises the risks substantially. Recent UK studies have failed to distinguish between first-time married, stepfamilies and the unmarried. For example, by combining first-time married and stepfamilies, a Home Office study undoubtedly under-reported the relative risks of domestic violence among other family types. Nevertheless, the additional risk in unmarried families was still twice as high, among single parents over twice as high, and among separated single mothers eleven times as high (Mirrlees-Black, 1999).

Unmarried couples and family outcomes

A common finding in studies of cohabiting people is that their behaviour and outcomes look much more like those of singles than those of married people. For example, cohabitee mortality rates are little different from those of singles (Lillard & Waite, 1995).

Cohabitee mental health is also similar to that of singles. One long-term study found that people became significantly less depressed only when they got married, and not when they started cohabiting (Lamb *et al.*, 2003). Cohabiting before getting married reduced this benefit. Another long-term study found that cohabitation was a strong predictor of male alcoholism, even after taking into account medical history and lifestyle attitudes. The study concluded that reductions in risky behaviour appear to occur *"only following marriage and not during cohabitation"* (Horwitz & White, 1998).

The cohabitee wage premium is roughly half that of married couples. Nor does it increase over time. Because marriages tend to last longer, so the relative returns of marriage increase with time (Daniel, 1995).

Children of cohabiting parents fare significantly less well at school than children of married couples, according to an Australian study that matched married and cohabiting couples for age, education, socio-economic status, personal attributes and relationship length (Sarantakos, 1996). US research concurs that children of cohabiting parents do less well – reduced academic performance, more school problems – after controlling for social, economic and parental factors. Cohabiting parents spend less time engaged with their children (McLanahan & Sandefur, 1994).

Children of cohabiting parents have higher mortality rates. In the UK, rates of infant mortality are 30–40% higher among cohabiting couples and 40–70% higher among single mothers, compared to children born to married couples. Rates of Sudden Infant Death Syndrome are three times and five to nine times higher respectively (ONS, 1999).

There is some evidence that selection is at work here, at least in part. Those who are more likely to cohabit include the poor, the affluent and those with a baby (Ermisch & Francesconi, 1998), women who value their career and men who value their leisure (Clarkberg *et al.*, 1995), those with divorced parents and those whose parents have a liberal attitude to divorce (Axinn & Thornton, 1992; Kiernan, 1999). So economics, parenthood, personal attitudes and family background are all influences. Nonetheless, the fact remains that unmarried families do less well.

Why getting divorced or splitting up is generally a bad idea

The consequences of relationship breakdown are high. Adults face greatly increased risks to their well-being, health and wealth following divorce or separation. Their children also face consequences that can affect them profoundly throughout their life. Marriage tends to take people out of poverty whereas divorce tends to take them into it.

According to a report by Family Matters Institute for a parliamentary group, relationship breakdown costs the UK taxpayer a minimum of £15 billion every year (Lindsay *et al.*, 2000). That equates to one quarter of the entire National Health Service bill or around £11 paid by every taxpayer every week. Most of this cost involves support for single parents. Another large chunk goes towards the additional education, health and crime costs that can be directly attributed to family breakdown.

In stark contrast, £5 million per year is spent on support for marriage and prevention of relationship breakdown (www.dfes.gov.uk). After spending £570 per year picking up the pieces of family breakdown, the UK taxpayer contributes just 19p trying to prevent things from getting worse.

Things are not getting better. In fact family breakdown, i.e. the formation of one-parent families, grew at a rate of 2.5% per year between 1995 and 2000 (Haskey, 2002). The engine of this growth is the break-up of unmarried families.

Things are guaranteed to get worse. With unmarried cohabitation increasingly the norm, 40% of babies born in the UK are now born to unmarried parents (www.statistics.gov.uk). Yet cohabiting parents are also four to five times more likely than married parents to separate, leaving far more children than ever before to face the many increased risks to health and wealth outlined below.

The media focus easily on divorce and marriage because those are the figures that are published. Yet the really big story now is that three out of every four young children experiencing family breakdown have unmarried parents.

It's not divorce that is driving family breakdown. It's the break-up of unmarried families.

This is a major public health and wealth issue. Unless the rates of both divorce and cohabitation are stabilised and reversed, and marriage reinforced, the associated costs are guaranteed to continue skyrocketing indefinitely.

Consequences of divorce for children

It is well known that blacks in the US do worse than whites. Children from single-parent black families are twice as likely to be poor as children from two-parent black families. What is less well known is that the same is true of white families.

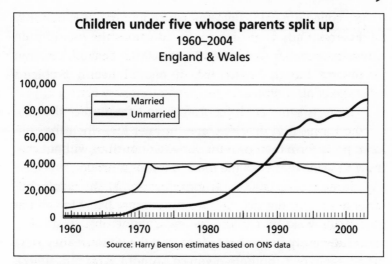

Figure 10.9 Children of separated parents

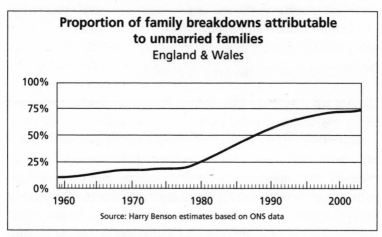

Figure 10.10 Family breakdown by status

Almost all the difference in poverty rates is due not to race, but to marital status and welfare dependency (Rector *et al.*, 2001).

Not only does family breakdown cause poverty, it causes ill health. Children's emotional well-being plummets following so-called amicable divorces, which represent the majority of divorces. Only after high-conflict divorces, the minority, do children do better (Amato & Booth, 2001). Overall, children of divorce face a higher risk of mental health problems (Cherlin *et al.*, 1998).

There is some evidence from long-term studies that the greatest impact of divorce comes in later life, when the children try to form their own intimate relationships without ever having seen what even the most ordinary marriage looks like (Wallerstein *et al.*, 2000). Perhaps not surprisingly, adult children of divorce are two to three times more likely to cohabit and, if they do marry, are far more vulnerable to divorce, especially early in their marriage and the younger they were when their own parents divorced (Amato & Booth, 1997). Studies in the UK and elsewhere also show a strong link between parental divorce and later criminal behaviour (Farrington, 1990; Sampson, 1992).

Consequences of divorce for adults

Adults who split up also face a range of greatly increased risks, to health, mortality and wealth. Incidences of alcoholism, depression, any psychiatric disorder, and suicide are all about twice as likely among most or all categories of unmarried people as among the married (Robins & Reiger, 1991; Smith *et al.*, 1988). Mortality rates are higher among adult children of divorce (Singh & Yu, 1996; Tucker *et al.*, 1997). Household income typically collapses following divorce as wage earners become less productive, homemakers are disadvantaged when they return to the labour market, divorce drains savings and two homes are required (Corcoran, 1994). It is easy to understand why half of all divorcing households move into poverty and single parents are several times more likely to be poor (Heath & Kiker, 1992; McLanahan & Sandefur, 1994).

A caveat on research

Having loaded up on the doom and gloom, it's vital to remember that being in a statistically high-risk group does not condemn an individual to that fate. Most kids of divorce do OK. Here are some of the factors that could put me personally at a high risk of divorce:

- My parents divorced when I was three, which increases my own risk of divorce by 50–100%
- I flew Commando helicopters in the Falklands War. Experience of combat raises my risk of divorce by 60%
- Because my wife, Kate, and I lived together intermittently before we got engaged, that raises our risk by 40–85% (although 18 years later we may be safe from that one now)
- Various interpersonal behaviours, such as a tendency to take things personally and withdraw when faced with domestic conflict, also increase my risk of divorce
- Having a large family of six children reduces my likelihood of a satisfying marriage
- This excludes all the other risks to which I am more exposed as a child of divorce in terms of crime, education, health and well-being problems.

The good news is that I don't have to live with the additional divorce risks posed by having different values and beliefs, being in a second marriage, having a defensive personality, having poor problem-solving skills, or having a low level of commitment.

In the end, this kind of research only gives me a better understanding of the risks. All of us are individuals. Either I can let the risk factors swamp me, or I can decide to take charge of my own marriage and beat the odds.

Marriage works

Marriage may well be in decline as we react against the rise in divorces and try to find a better alternative. Yet the hard truth is that we are misleading ourselves badly by turning our backs on it. The last decade of research confirms overwhelmingly the wisdom of the past and the foolishness of our present path.

Marriage is good for us. Marriage works. The mindset and behaviour that accompany marriage produce all sorts of social benefits and protections that cohabitation and divorce typically do not. Married people are more stable, happier, healthier and wealthier, and live longer than any category of unmarried people. Of course there are powerful exceptions to this statement. There are bad marriages just as there are good un-marriages and sensible divorces. But the exceptions do not make the rule. We reject marriage at our peril.

The links between marriage and subsequent benefits and between cohabitation or divorce and subsequent risks are now as clear as the link between smoking and subsequent cancer. Governments put health warnings on cigarettes to reduce smoking. When will they take steps to reduce cohabitation and divorce?

References
- Amato, P. and Booth, A. (1997) *A Generation at Risk: Growing Up in an Era of Family Upheaval.* Cambridge, MA: Harvard University Press.

- Amato, P. and Booth, A. (2001) Parental predivorce relations and offspring postdivorce well-being. *Journal of Marriage and the Family* 63, 197–212.
- Axinn, W. and Thornton, A. (1992) The relationship between premarital cohabitation and divorce: Selectivity or causal influence? *Demography* 29, 357–374.
- Boheim, R. and Ermisch, J. (1999) *Breaking up – Financial surprises and partnership dissolution*. Paper presented at the Royal Economic Society Conference, Nottingham.
- Bumpass, L.L. and Sweet, J.A. (1995). Cohabitation, marriage and union stability: Preliminary findings from NSFH2. *NSFH Working Paper No. 65*. University of Wisconsin-Madison: Center for Demography and Ecology.
- Cherlin, A., Chase-Lansdale, P. and McRae, C. (1998) Effects of parental divorce on mental health throughout the life course. *American Sociological Review* 63, 239–249.
- Clarkberg, M., Stolzenberg, R. and Waite, L. (1995) Attitudes, values and entrance into cohabitational versus marital unions. *Social Forces* 74, 609–632.
- Corcoran, P. (1994) Unpublished paper. Survey Research Centre, University of Michigan.
- Daly, M. and Wilson, M. (1998) *The Truth about Cinderella: A Darwinian View of Parental Love*. London: Weidenfeld & Nicholson.
- Daniel, K. (1995) The marriage premium. In M.Tommasi and K. Ierulli, (eds) *The New Economics of Human Behaviour*, pp. 113–125. Cambridge: CUP.
- Davis, J.A. (1984) New money, an old man/lady, and two's company. *Social Indicators Research* 15, 319–350.
- Ermisch, J. (2002) *When forever is no more: Economic implications of changing family structure*. ISER, University of Essex.
- Ermisch, J. and Francesconi, M. (1998) *Cohabitation in Great Britain: Not for long, but here to stay*. ISER, University of Essex.

- Farrington, D.P. (1990) Implications of criminal career research for the prevention of offending. *Journal of Adolescence* 13, 93–113.
- Goodwin, J.S. *et al.* (1987) The effect of marital status on stage, treatment and survival of cancer patients. *Journal of the American Medical Association* 258, 3125–3130.
- Haskey, J. (1992) *Population Trends*.
- Haskey, J. (2002) One-parent families – and the dependent children living in them – in Great Britain. *Population Trends* 109, 46–57.
- Hayes, B.C. and Prior, P.M. (2003) The relationship between marital status and health. *Journal of Family Issues* 24, 124–148.
- Heath, J. and Kiker, B.F. (1992) Determinants of spells of poverty following divorce. *Review of Social Economy* 49, 305–315.
- Horwitz, A. and White, H. (1998) The relationship of cohabitation and mental health: A study of a young adult cohort. *Journal of Marriage and Family* 60, 505–514.
- Horwitz, A., White, H. and Howell-White, S. (1996) Becoming married and mental health: A longitudinal study of a cohort of young adults. *Journal of Marriage and Family* 58, 895–907.
- Kahn, J.R. and London, K.A. (1991) Premarital sex and the risk of divorce. *Journal of Marriage and Family* 53, 845–855.
- Kamp Dush, C., Cohan, C. and Amato, P. (2003) The relationship between cohabitation and marital quality and stability: Change across cohorts? *Journal of Marriage and Family* 65, 539–549.
- Kiernan, K. (1999) Childbearing outside marriage in Western Europe. *Population Trends* 98, ONS.
- Lamb, K.A., Lee, G.R. and DeMaris, A. (2003) Union formation and depression: Selection and relationship effects. *Journal of Marriage and Family* 65, 953–962.

- Lillard, L.A. and Waite, L.J. (1995) Till death do us part: Marital disruption and mortality. *American Journal of Sociology* 100, 1131–1156.
- Lindgren, (1997) Research centre on population, Helsinki. In J. Ditch, H. Barnes, J. Bradshaw (eds) *Developments in National Family Policies in 1996*. European Observatory on National Family Policies: University of York.
- Lindsay, D. *et al.* (2000) *The Cost of Family Breakdown*. Bedford: Family Matters Institute.
- Marks, N. and Lambert, J. (1998) Marital status continuity and change among young and midlife adults: Longitudinal effects on psychological well-being. *Journal of Family Issues* 19, 652–686.
- Marsh, A. and Perry, J. (2003) Family change 1999 to 2001. DWP Research report no. 181. CDS: Leeds.
- McLanahan, S. and Sandefur, G. (1994) *Growing Up With a Single Parent: What Hurts, What Helps*. Cambridge, MA: Harvard University Press.
- Mirrlees-Black, C. (1999) *Domestic Violence: Findings from a new British Crime Survey Self-completion Questionnaire*. London: Home Office.
- Murphy, M., Glaser, K. and Grundy, E. (1997) Marital status and long-term illness in Great Britain. *Journal of Marriage and Family* 59, 156–164.
- Office of National Statistics (1999) *Live Births and Infant Deaths by Marital Status, Parity (Within Marriage) and Type of Registration (Outside Marriage)*. London: HMSO.
- Rector, R., Johnson, K. and Fagan, F. (2001) *Understanding Differences in Black and White Child Poverty Rates*. Washington DC: Heritage Foundation.
- Robins, L. and Reiger, D. (1991) *Psychiatric Disorders in America: The Epidemiologic Catchment Area Study*. New York: Free Press.

- Sampson, R.J. (1992) Crime in cities: The effects of formal and informal social control. In M. Tonry and N. Morris (eds) *Crime and Justice*. Chicago: University of Chicago Press.
- Sarantakos, S. (1996) Children in three contexts: Family education and social development. *Children Australia* 21.
- Schoeni, R. (1995) Marital status and earnings in developed countries. *Journal of Population Economics* 8, 351–359.
- Singh, G. and Yu, S. (1996) US childhood mortality, 1950 through 1993: Trends and socioeconomic differentials. *American Journal of Public Health* 85, 505–512.
- Smith, J.C., Mercy, J.A. and Conn, J.M (1988) Marital status and the risk of suicide. *American Journal of Public Health* 78, 78–80.
- Smith, J.P. (1995) *Marriage, Assets and Savings*. Rand Corp.
- Teachman, J. (2003) Premarital sex, premarital cohabitation, and the risk of dissolution among women. *Journal of Marriage and Family* 65, 444–455.
- Tucker, J. *et al.* (1997) Parental divorce: Effects on individual behavior and longevity. *Journal of Personality and Social Psychology* 73, 385–386.
- Waite, L. and Gallagher, M. (2000) *The Case for Marriage*. New York: Doubleday.
- Wallerstein, J., Lewis, J. and Blakelee, S. (2000) *The Unexpected Legacy of Divorce: A 25-year Landmark Study*. New York: Hyperion.
- Whelan, R. (1994) *Broken Homes and Battered Children: A Study of the Relationship Between Child Abuse and Family Type*. Oxford: Family Education Trust.

Chapter 11 **The case for marriage education**

In this chapter

- The factors that make marriage succeed or fail
- The importance of both positive and negative factors
- Programmes that work

Can we make marriages work better?

Having accepted that the case for supporting marriage is compelling, the next question to be asked is *"Can we help make marriages better and prevent them from getting worse?"*

Everybody has an opinion about what makes marriage work. Typical answers include good communication, love, commitment, compromise, hard work, time, luck, friendship, being soulmates. Yet there is no reason why public opinion should be right. What people *do* is more important than what they say. One of the earliest marriage researchers made this wise observation: *"Studying what people say about themselves is no substitute for studying how they behave. Questionnaires and scales of marital satisfaction and dissatisfaction have yielded very little. We need to look at what people do with one another"* (Rausch *et al.*, 1974).

In the decades since then, especially in the 1990s, an astonishing amount of progress has been made. Perhaps the most remarkable finding is that researchers can discriminate with up to 90% accuracy between those who will divorce and those who will end up happily married in five years' time. This has been done either through observing how a couple behave (Gottman & Levenson, 2000) or through analysing the level of couple agreement across a range of topics in an inventory (Fowers & Olson, 1989). The result is a number of different approaches to marriage education.

If we know what predicts future success and failure, we ought to be able to teach people how to "do" marriage better. An especially important observation from this research is that it's the negative ways we hurt one another that are the biggest determinants of whether we stay together or not. The positive things we share and do well together tend to determine whether we are happy. These are not opposites. We need to teach both and not assume that telling people how to communicate well is enough to stop people from hurting one another.

Do marriage education courses work? The straight answer is "yes". We can be very confident that couples tend to become happier in their marriages after doing a course of marriage education. Recent research reviews provide more than enough evidence (Jakubowski *et al.*, 2004; Carroll & Doherty, 2003).

But the research is less certain when it comes to steering couples away from divorce. There is evidence that marriage education can do this, but it is far from comprehensive. The proverbial glass can therefore be seen as half full or half empty when it comes to the effectiveness of marriage education. Marriage education works, but the research has some way to go to carry the sceptics.

As with the previous chapter, support couples really only need to understand these basic ideas rather than worry about the detail. If you want to know more about how and why marriage education appears to be most effective, read on. I've tried to interpret the research in non-technical language that fairly represents the broad thrust of things. Researchers themselves will doubtless want to qualify my simplifications. Yet without such simplifications, research can come across as unintelligible and contradictory.

Putting together effective marriage education

There are two main routes to discovering what makes marriages work. We can start at the beginning of a marriage and look forwards at what happens. Or we can start later on and look backwards at what has already happened.

Retrospective research involves asking married couples about the marriage they have already had. This can provide great insight when we want to know why long-term marriages have lasted so long. But there is a major disadvantage in that this insight is reliant on memory. An example of how this can be distorted is in the so-called U-curve of marriage. When people look back retrospectively on their marriages, they say they started off happy, became less happy as their children arrived and grew up, and got happy again when the little darlings left home. Unfortunately, the U-curve disappears when couples are followed over time and asked how they are doing along the way (Vaillant & Vaillant, 1993).

Prospective research, on the other hand, starts with the assumption that there are factors present today that influence our odds of future success. All sorts of information on couples can be measured objectively. Over time, we can then compare the successful and unsuccessful marriages and try to find initial differences.

The premise of marriage education is to change the way

married couples think and behave using these known factors. We can then evaluate the success or otherwise of different approaches.

Predicting marriage outcome with 80–90% accuracy

Let's start by looking at risk factors – those background factors or ways we do things that make us more likely to succeed or fail. John Gottman is a leading professor of marriage research in the US. Couples go into his "love lab" and sit in front a video camera while they discuss a contentious issue. Just three minutes of this appears to be enough for him to say whether their odds are good or not of making it through the next five years. By comparing the behaviour of hundreds of couples on video with how their marriages turned out years later, Gottman has identified particular behaviours to watch out for.

Gottman's analysts keep score of all sorts of things the couples do and say – their timing, their eye contact, their use of language, their body language, their tone of voice, how they respond to each other. These subtle behaviours are hard to pick up unless you know exactly what to look for. The result is the claim that he can predict with 80–90% accuracy how happy they will be in five years' time, as well as whether they will still be together. And that is all from a three-minute video (Carrere & Gottman, 1999). Amazing!

Other researchers have done much the same thing using questionnaires or inventories. An inventory is simply a shopping list of statements, discussed in more detail in Chapter 6. The results, however, look similar. Profiles of how much couples agree with one another across a range of topics can be used to predict with 80–90% accuracy how happy and stable they will be in future years (Fowers & Olson, 1986).

Not all researchers are convinced about these findings. Several are, rightly in my view, sceptical about predictions. A formula that works for one group doesn't work nearly as well for another group (Clements *et al.*, 2004). There are too many other background and environmental factors (Bradbury & Karney, 2004). And in any case it simply doesn't work if you try to guess whether any one couple are heading for a life of bliss or had best give up now (Ebling & Levenson, 2003). What a relief!

The bottom line, however, is that we can be very confident about the risk factors that make marriages more likely to succeed or fail.

Predictors of marital stability

The factors that predict happiness do not necessarily predict divorce. Howard Markman and Scott Stanley at the University of Denver helpfully arrange the factors that predict whether a couple will stay together or divorce into two groups (Markman *et al.*, 2001).

The first group are *"static"* factors. These are fixed things we can't do much about. They include *defensive personality, parental divorce, prior cohabitation, prior divorce, previous children, different religious beliefs, marrying young, whirlwind romances, and serious financial difficulties*. For example, if your parents divorced, you face a higher divorce risk than those whose parents stayed married.

The second group are *"dynamic"* factors. These are changeable things we can do something about. They include *a negative style of communication, difficulty with handling disagreements, unrealistic beliefs about marriage, different attitudes about important things, and a low level of commitment to each other*. For example, if you enter marriage thinking your spouse "will make me whole", you are more likely to divorce than those who have more realistic beliefs.

There are two important conclusions. What we learn as we grow up influences us deeply. But the patterns of behaviour we develop within our relationship are also vital. Couples who stay married tend to have fewer negative automatic interactions, or bad habits. Couples who divorce tend to have more. My list of STOP signs in Chapter 3 is based on *"Escalation, Invalidation, Negative Interpretations, and Withdrawal"* (Markman *et al.*, 2001) and *"Criticism, Contempt, Defensiveness, and Stonewalling"* (Gottman, 1994).

It is striking that all of these predictive factors are negatives – things that have been done badly. Positive factors – things that have been done well – are far less powerful predictors of marital stability. In other words, it's the negative aspects of our background as well as the extent to which we handle our differences negatively that best predict marital success or failure.

Therefore, in order to improve "stability", we must think of marriage education as an attempt to reduce these negative factors or bad habits. I discussed this in Chapters 3 and 4.

Predictors of marital satisfaction

It should be no great surprise to discover that "marital stability" and "marital satisfaction" are not necessarily the same. Most of us know of seemingly unhappy couples who stay together. We also know of seemingly happy couples who split up.

A good example of this is what happens when couples have a baby. Marital satisfaction tends to deteriorate. This won't be much of a surprise to exhausted parents of young children. It's hard to find the energy to be excited about each other when we're so exhausted by daily life. Yet in these early years, new parents are also less likely to get divorced than at other times (Waite & Lillard, 1991). The constant demand of babies allows little opportunity to think of life away from each other.

The predictors of marital satisfaction also tend to fall into static and dynamic groups. The *"static"* factors that make future happiness more likely mostly concern the *positive aspects of a couple's background*. For example, one major survey found that happy couples are far more likely to say they have a good personality match and shared beliefs and values (Olson & Olson-Sigg, 2000).

The *"dynamic"* factors that make future happiness more likely mostly concern the *positive ways couples handle their differences*. For example, the same survey found that happy couples are far more likely to communicate well, handle differences well, discuss problems well, show affection to each other, and agree how to spend their time and money together. Other studies show that, even when skill levels are poor, couples are happy provided they show positive affect for one another – i.e. they are nice, funny and interested (Bradbury & Karney, 2004).

Therefore, in order to improve "satisfaction", we should now be thinking of marriage education as an attempt to build up these positive factors. I discussed this in Chapter 5.

Stability *and* satisfaction

A simplified working summary of research findings might thus look something like this:

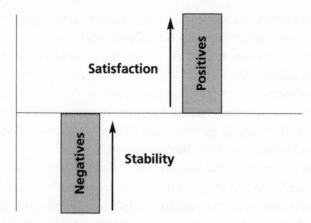

Figure 11.1 Stability and satisfaction

- *"Stability"* depends largely on the *negative* aspects of family background and the extent to which couples handle their differences *negatively*
- *"Satisfaction"* depends largely on the positive aspects of family background and the extent to which couples handle their differences *positively*.

Although this simple model holds true in general, there is some overlap. For example, the presence of negative factors in the early years of marriage is the best guide to whether a couple will stay together. But, in later years, the absence of positive factors "eventually takes its toll" as the better predictor (Gottman & Levenson, 2000). A marriage without negative STOP signs can survive many years. But without positive strokes, the marriage eventually wears down and dies.

Positives *and* negatives

An obvious question now arises as to whether a course that concentrates on building up the good things in marriage –

raising levels of "satisfaction" – will also be effective at reducing the bad things that influence "stability".

In some cases, negative and positive are not opposites. Having divorced parents (negative) predicts instability. Having married parents (positive) predicts little. Likewise, a low level of commitment (negative) predicts instability. A high level of commitment (positive) predicts little. A note at the end of the chapter explains this.

Some positive and negative factors do overlap. Couples who communicate poorly are more likely to be unstable. Couples who communicate well are more likely to be satisfied. Much the same applies to the handling of disagreements. But it is wrong to assume that teaching positive communication and conflict-resolution skills will increase stability and satisfaction. There are times when we communicate well and times when we communicate poorly. There will be times when we handle our disagreements well and times when we handle them badly. Learning one doesn't necessarily get rid of the other. We still have both.

Teaching positive skills and satisfaction may or may not have a corresponding impact by default on negative factors and stability. Positives and negatives are separate factors that are sometimes related and sometimes not. Our best bet is to make sure we cover both.

The "myth" of marital happiness

This key distinction between stability and satisfaction is complicated in everyday life because of a widespread and persistent belief that happy couples do stay together (Fowers, 2000). Almost all couples, when asked, rate their own marriage in terms of their ability to communicate. In fact researchers find it virtually impossible to separate happiness and communication (Fowers & Olson, 1993).

This explains in large part why so many marriage education courses are overwhelmingly focused on the importance of positive communication. Good communication is undoubtedly important for improving marital satisfaction. But teaching good communication doesn't necessarily help people stay together.

Researchers contest the issue of communication vigorously. Some argue that "active listening" skills are hardly ever used by real couples in everyday life, their use predicts nothing, they have little effect on behaviour in outcome studies, and they are hard to use when you most need them – i.e. when you are angry, tired or upset (Gottman et al., 1998). Others argue that the whole point of "active listening" skills is not to make people happier, but to make it less likely they will hurt one another (Stanley et al., 2000). I can relate to both these views.

We can now look at any marriage education programme aware of a major caveat:

- Teaching mostly *positive communication* skills will not necessarily reduce the negative automatic behaviours that predict instability.

Do marriage courses work?

Finding out whether marriage education courses actually do what they are supposed to do is extraordinarily difficult to achieve (Halford, 2000; Stanley, 2001).

Firstly, it's hard to make comparisons because there are so many different types of course. Some courses arise from research, others from experience. Some courses span a weekend or a few evenings, others just a few hours. Some courses are done at home or one to one, others in groups. Some courses focus on information, others teach skills.

Secondly, we're not very good at evaluating courses. We tend to think highly of any course if we paid for it, were reasonably comfortable, and enjoyed the presentation. Consistently positive feedback may simply reflect these factors rather than whether the course is actually any good.

Thirdly, we're not very good at evaluating our own marriages. We tend to tell people our marriage is *"better than average"* to begin with. Regardless of the fact that not everybody can be better than average, it can be hard to improve on such a good start.

Fourthly, the "dynamic" factors that influence couple stability are subtle, reflecting body language, eye contact, and the way words are used. These nuances are generally not picked up by couples themselves but by trained observers carefully analysing videos of couple interactions. These kinds of studies are both expensive and time-consuming.

Finally, putting together a study that compares couples who do a course with couples who don't is very difficult. It's hard to make sure that the couples who do the course aren't the kind of people who would have done well anyway. This is called a "selection effect". It's also hard to keep track of the couples who didn't do the course. Most likely those who can't be traced have split up. But that can't be assumed. So there is a problem with "attrition" between groups.

Nonetheless, many courses have been evaluated – for better, for worse. They can be described in terms of three general course types (Halford, 2000). I find that understanding the distinction between stability and satisfaction helps me accept why different courses have different effects.

1. "Information & Awareness courses"

These courses seek to raise awareness, dispel myths and generally impart helpful information and insight about marriage. The nature of these courses tends to be eclectic, personal and non-standardised.

Typical subject matter might include the "love languages", "emotional needs", "marriage maps", "sexuality", "in-laws", "money", and simple exercises in "communication" and "conflict resolution". We looked at some of these ideas in Chapter 5.

Many small-scale studies have found that this type of course helps improve self-reported marital satisfaction in the short term. This suggests that courses are successful in building up the key positive factors. But, in all cases, there is no comparison group or follow-up beyond six months.

Nor is there any evidence that these courses reduce divorce rates. This may seem surprising, given the claims sometimes made about such courses. It's less surprising considering the lack of attention to the all-important negative factors.

2. "Inventories"

Three research-based inventories (or questionnaires) are available worldwide – FOCCUS, PREPARE and RELATE. These are personalised awareness-raising courses facilitated by an individual or a couple. An inventory consists of a standardised list of statements based on subjects or domains that predict marital outcomes. A profile is then produced based on the degree of agreement within the couple on each subject.

A number of studies have found that these profiles can be remarkably accurate predictors of both satisfaction and stability up to five years later. This means that the inventories are covering the right territory – in terms of both positive and negative factors. Evidence from programme originators suggests that 10–15% of all couples choose to defer or cancel their weddings after completing the inventory. These couples have similar profiles to those who end up unhappy or divorced.

Although there are no published outcome studies to tell us whether inventories improve marriage or not, they do seem to reduce divorce rates by weeding out many of those destined for divorce.

3. "Skills courses"
These are structured programmes involving teaching, demonstration and coaching of the skills that predict marital outcomes. Three courses of this type have been studied: "Relationship Enhancement" (RE), "Couple Communication" (CC), and the "Prevention & Relationship Enhancement Programme" (PREP).

Studies comparing RE with "Information & Awareness"-type courses find that RE is the more successful at increasing marital satisfaction. RE's main goal is to build "empathy".

PREP's twin goals are to reduce negative behaviours and to increase positive behaviours (Markman *et al.*, 2001). Almost all of the best comparison studies involve PREP. Four of these PREP studies – in the US, Germany and Australia – showed increases in marital satisfaction. Three of them have shown substantial reductions in divorce rates of between 50 and 80% up to five years later. Two other studies of PREP, both of which have methodological shortcomings that make them hard to interpret, found no apparent benefits (Stanley, 2001).

What about other courses?

Aside from inventories, few of the better-known marriage education courses have been subjected to much or any rigorous research to tell us whether they work or not.

For example, "Marriage Encounter" weekends involve the intensive learning and practice of communication skills. These skills are intended to facilitate a deeper level of mutual commitment. Nonetheless, Marriage Encounter differs from a pure *"skills"* course in that it covers less ground but with far greater intensity. Although there are 16 known studies, none are of sufficient rigour to allow useful conclusions to be drawn.

Nicky and Sila Lee's fast-growing "The Marriage Course", based in the UK, covers a broad range of issues and processes relevant to marriage. This covers a lot more ground than a pure *"information and awareness"* course but is less focused than a pure *"skills"* course. No studies have yet been conducted of this course. It's not especially obvious how or whether either of these courses fits into the above categories.

In any case, there is a dearth of good-quality research. Reviews of existing research mention just four marriage education programmes that been evaluated to a minimum standard, and only seven individual studies that use reliable techniques (Jakubowski *et al.*, 2004; Carroll & Doherty, 2003). The sort of controlled observational studies conducted on the likes of PREP cost hundreds of thousands of pounds or dollars. Top-quality research is therefore highly dependent on government funding sources.

What marriage courses need to cover

There have already been a great many attempts to teach marriage, few of which have been well evaluated. However, there is more than enough evidence that the quality of a marriage can be boosted and some evidence that divorce rates can be reduced. This provides ammunition for both critics and supporters alike. But we don't need to wait for expensive outcome studies, provided we use what the research tells us already:

- Background family-of-origin issues influence future marriage outcomes
- Interactive couple behaviour – affection, communication, conflict resolution, commitment, values, beliefs – also influences future marriage outcomes
- Positive behaviours have most influence on our quality of marriage
- Negative behaviours have most influence on our risk of divorce
- Learning positive behaviours may not cancel out negative behaviours. We need to learn both
- To be confident of improving marriage, virtually any course makes some difference
- To be confident of reducing divorce, we need to be more specific. We can use inventories as a filter. We can raise awareness of negative behaviours as well as positive ones. We can teach and coach practical skills that reduce these negative behaviours.

Note

While coming from a broken home makes it more likely that I will end up divorced, coming from a stable home doesn't improve my odds by the equivalent amount. I've been asked many times how this can be. It's not intuitively obvious. The answer is all in the maths and the proportions.

Let's say a random group of 100 people get married. Twenty of them come from broken homes and 80 from stable homes. Fifty of them end up divorced, i.e. half. If getting divorced does not depend on your background, we should find that half of the 20 from broken homes and half of the 80 from stable homes get divorced.

Suppose we find that fifteen from broken homes and 35 from stable homes get divorced. For those from broken homes, we expected ten divorces and got fifteen. That makes the risk factor 50% higher (15/10) than it should be. For those from a stable home, we expected 40 divorces and got 35. That makes the risk factor 12.5% lower (35/40) than it should be.

If people from broken homes get divorced more than they should, the odds will always be three times higher because there are three times fewer of them in the first place. The question is then whether those odds are large enough to be meaningful and unlikely to be due to chance.

A 50% increase in divorce risk for those from broken homes is both significant and large. A 13% reduction in divorce risk for those from stable homes is not.

References

- Bradbury, T. and Karney, B. (2004) Understanding and altering the longitudinal course of marriage. *Journal of Marriage and Family* 66, 862–879.

- Carrere, S. and Gottman, J. (1999) Predicting divorce among newlyweds from the first three minutes of a marital conflict discussion. *Family Process* 38, 293–301.
- Carroll, J. and Doherty, W. (2003) Evaluating the effectiveness of premarital prevention programs: A meta-analytic review of outcome research. *Family Relations* 52, 105–118.
- Clements, M., Stanley, S. and Markman, H. (2004) Before they said "I do": Discriminating among marital outcomes over 13 years. *Journal of Marriage and Family* 66, 613–626.
- Ebling, R. and Levenson, R.W. (2003) Who are the marital experts? *Journal of Marriage and Family* 65, 130–142.
- Fowers, B.J. (2000) *Beyond the Myth of Marital Happiness*. San Francisco: Jossey Bass.
- Fowers, B.J. and Olson, D.H. (1986) Predicting marital success with PREPARE: A predictive validity study. *Journal of Marital and Family Therapy* 12, 403–413.
- Fowers, B.J. and Olson, D.H. (1989) ENRICH marital inventory: A discriminant validity and cross-validity assessment. *Journal of Marital and Family Therapy* 15, 65–79.
- Fowers, B.J. and Olson, D.H. (1993) ENRICH marital satisfaction scale: A reliability and validity study. *Journal of Family Psychology* 7, 1–10.
- Gottman, J. (1994) *Why Marriages Succeed or Fail*. New York: Simon & Schuster.
- Gottman, J., Coan, J., Carrere, S. and Swanson, C. (1998) Predicting marital happiness and stability from newlywed interactions. *Journal of Marriage and Family* 60, 5–22.
- Gottman, J. and Levenson, R. (2000) The timing of divorce: Predicting when a couple will divorce over a 14-year period. *Journal of Marriage and Family* 62, 737–745.
- Halford, W.K. (2000) *Australian Couples in Millenium Three*. Canberra: Australian Department of Family and Community Services.

- Jakubowski, S., Milne, E., Brunner, H. and Miller, R. (2004) A review of empirically supported marital enrichment programs. *Family Relations* 53, 528–536.
- Markman, H.J., Stanley, S.M. and Blumberg, S.L. (2001) *Fighting for Your Marriage, New & Revised.* San Francisco: Wiley.
- Olson, D.H. and Olson-Sigg, A. (2000) *Empowering Couples: Building on Your Strengths.* Canada: ENRICH.
- Rausch, H.L. *et al.* (1974) *Communication, Conflict and Marriage.* San Fancisco: Jossey-Bass.
- Stanley, S.M. (2001) Making the case for premarital education. *Family Relations* 50, 272–280.
- Stanley, S., Bradbury, T. and Markman, H. (2000) Structural flaws in the bridge from basic research on marriage to interventions for couples. *Journal of Marriage and Family* 62, 256–264.
- Vaillant, C.O. and Vaillant, G.E. (1993) Is the U-curve of marital satisfaction an illusion? A 40-year study of marriage. *Journal of Marriage and Family* 55, 230–239.
- Waite, L. and Lillard, L. (1991) Children and marital disruption. *American Journal of Sociology* 96, 930–953.

Chapter 12 **The case for mentoring**

In this chapter

- Why the case for couple counselling is so weak
- Why the case for mentoring is so much more compelling

Extended family – Values, Learning and Support

After my parents divorced in the early 1960s, much of my childhood was spent growing up alongside my extended family. The result was that I saw the way other people did marriage and family up close. Some of it was for the better, some for the worse. But all of it enlarged my experience of what works and what doesn't. From my extended family, I learned what was important, I learned how we did things and I learned how we supported one another. All these things I've taken into my adult life, often accepting them unquestioningly until I see somebody else doing things differently.

In Chapter 1, I pointed out the huge progress we have made in the areas of freedom, choice and mobility. Yet the cost of this progress has been high in terms of what we have lost. As we move away from extended family networks, we lose our sense of interdependence and values. We lose the role models from whom we learn how to do or not to do family. We lose our support systems that look after us when things go

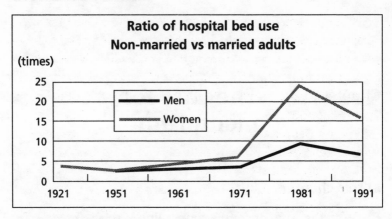

Figure 12.1 Hospital bed use and marital status

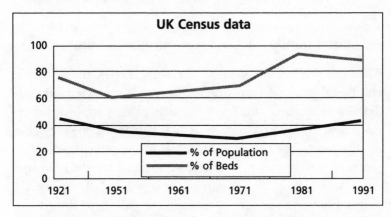

Figure 12.2 Hospital bed use by unmarried adults (lower line represents share of population)

wrong – when we have relationship problems, when we get ill or when we merely grow old. I think we are the worse for it as a society.

There is specific evidence that the support and responsibilities previously provided by extended families have now shifted to the state. For example, since the 1970s the proportion of unmarried men and women occupying UK hospital beds has rocketed upward (Prior & Hayes, 2003); 90% of all hospital or care-home bed occupants are unmarried. Most of that increase has come from single young people and single older widows, almost certainly reflecting their lack of extended family support. With freedom and mobility can come isolation.

Many people are beginning to realise that we need to replace and deliberately rebuild the concept of role models and support. Inner-city schools have started applying the concept of mentoring, with some success. A March 2003 article in *The Times* newspaper quotes a head teacher as saying *"What really did it for us was being able to invest in learning mentors"*. Another head teacher talks of the benefits brought by working adults acting as mentors to twelve-year-olds. In industry, mentoring or apprenticeships have long been the norm, although often stifled nowadays by employment red tape.

Despite this, apprenticeship and mentoring are still the norm in some fields. The popular chef Jamie Oliver was discussing with TV interviewer Michael Parkinson how he had become so expert at his trade. *"Mentors is the key,"* he said.

Mentoring is the beautifully simple idea that we learn from those with more experience. In the past, we had extended family. Mentoring for couples is essentially an attempt to provide the benefits of extended family that we have lost.

Marriage mentoring provides couples starting out with a clear sense of values, an opportunity to learn alongside those who have made marriage work, and an opportunity to build the kind of close-knit friendship that allows couples to nip problems in the bud. Mentoring is extended family by another name.

However, for couples the concept of mentoring is still

fairly alien. People don't talk couple to couple as a matter of routine. When we have problems, we look to counsellors. Counselling is what we think of most when we think about support for marriage or couples.

I want to start, therefore, by looking at how and why couple counselling is not all it's cracked up to be. The irony is that much of the couple-counselling industry explicitly rejects the three central principles of value, learning and support. Studies confirm that couple counselling is not effective.

This interpretation may offend some of those with a heavy investment in couple counselling. Yet I hope it will free other couple counsellors who wonder about their industry's sacred cows. Much more importantly, I hope it will free the vast majority of ordinary married couples who want to make a difference as support couples. You don't have to be an expert to help others with their marriage or relationships.

The relative failure of couple counselling

So why am I negative about couple counselling? I'm not talking about one-to-one counselling, which I rate highly. The answer is that I think the whole couple-counselling model is deeply flawed and not simply a valid alternative. I see little evidence to support the methods generally employed in couple counselling. I see little evidence of successful outcomes as a result of couple counselling. I see unchallenged assumptions that have distorted the way family and relationship support is viewed and conducted. And I hear too many stories of awful experiences of couple counsellors. The positive stories seem to be a tiny minority.

I'm not the first person to think this. Far better-informed researchers are well ahead of me. For example, top American therapist and researcher Bill Doherty says that most people go to couple counselling looking for structure and answers. But this is not what they get in practice (Doherty, 1999). They get:

- a neutral attitude to marriage – *"Stay married, get divorced, whatever works for you"*
- a focus on individual happiness – *"Follow your heart; trust your feelings; do what's best for you; if you're happy, so will the kids be happy"*
- a language that reflects consumer interests rather than family interests – *"It's not working any more; you deserve better; you have needs and rights; it's time to move on"*.

This has now filtered down to become the kind of tosh we hear in the media or in soaps. Couples go looking for a solution to their problem. They come away with the impression their marriage is the problem.

Is it reasonable to be neutral about marriage? No, because there are consequences. Take smoking as an example. Researchers have long shown that smoking is unhealthy and linked to cancer. The government advises us not to smoke and penalises smokers through taxes. Smoking is discouraged, penalised and restricted, but not completely banned. Those who wish to smoke have at least some freedom to do so. But nobody pretends that smoking is without consequence, as was the case in the 1960s and 1970s. We know what we are letting ourselves in for.

Exactly the same argument applies to marriage and divorce. Staying married is generally the better option for both adults and children. To be neutral is to pretend that both choices are equally valid. This is an irresponsible cop-out.

A further assumption is that those *"trapped in unhappy marriages"* are better off getting divorced. I've just read an interview in *The Times* newspaper with a well-respected head teacher who made exactly this claim.

The first major study to challenge this assumption found quite the opposite effect. The study, led by University of Chicago Professor Linda Waite (Waite *et al.*, 2002), was based on a two-stage survey of 5,000 adults in the late 1980s and early 1990s. The first interesting finding was that the concept of *"unhappy marriage"* is largely a myth. It turned out that 75% of the 645 people who said they were unhappy had happy spouses. So, most of the time, we're dealing with unhappy *people* and not unhappy marriages.

Waite then looked at what those initially unhappy people said about their marriage five years later. She found plenty of evidence that people became happier if they stayed married and no evidence that they became happier if they divorced. In fact, two-thirds of those who initially said they were *"unhappy"* reported being happily married five years later. More remarkably, 80% of the *"very unhappy"* people ended up happily married. The couples who divorced did not typically end up happier, less depressed or feeling more in control of their lives. This was true even after the authors took into account any possible effects of race, age, gender or income. So should you *"follow your heart"* and get out when things are bad? In the vast majority of cases, the best answer appears to be *"no"*.

Of course, the reality is that some marriages may be better off if brought to a close – for example where there is persistent abuse, violence or infidelity. This is true for the minority of divorces. Professors Alan Booth and Paul Amato have followed the progress of 2,000 US couples and their children for 20 years. They found that well over half of those couples who divorced along the way were indistinguishable only a year or two beforehand from those couples who stayed married, in terms of couples' reported well-being and levels of conflict.

The most remarkable finding from their study relates to the so-called "amicable" divorce. Children of low-conflict couples suffered a collapse in their reported well-being following the divorce, as the chart shows. In contrast, the children of the high-conflict couples did markedly better following divorce (Booth & Amato, 2001). A June 2003 survey published in the *Guardian* found that 60% of UK divorces were *"amicable"*, suggesting that UK and US divorce data regarding conflict are fairly similar.

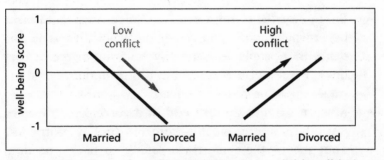

Figure 12.3 Effect of conflict and divorce on child well-being

Undoubtedly, some people come to counsellors wanting somebody in authority to empathise with them and to rubber-stamp their decision to divorce. But most people want a solution to their marriage problems. Therefore, the final question to ask is whether couple counselling actually makes any difference. The evidence is not compelling.

A major review paper by Professor John Gottman looked at various approaches to couple counselling and their outcomes (Gottman, 1998). He concluded this: *"First, if one requires replicated effects, treatment gains are not generally maintained over time. Second, it does not seem to matter very much what one does in treatment. In general effect sizes are the same, regardless of the exact nature of the intervention. ...they suggest the conclusion that any of the parts equals the whole. Furthermore, it appears possible that all parts may be as effective as...an approach based on an erroneous assumption about what makes marriages work. If this remarkable conclusion were true, almost all marital treatment effects would be due to non-specifics such as trust in the therapist, hope, the existence of a structured program, all of which could be considered placebo effects."*

The typical value-free, non-prescriptive approach is therefore flawed for three main reasons:

- **Being married is not a neutral choice.** Most families do better when married than when divorced. There is no evidence that people are generally better off divorced. This doesn't rule out the possibility that a minority of marriages might be better off ended.
- **Most marriages needn't end in divorce.** Most divorces are amicable and emerge from low-conflict marriages. That means these marriages ought to be salvageable even up to quite a late stage. The overwhelming majority of those who stick out their marriages find ways to become happier.
- **Most divorces are dreadful for children.** The majority of divorces are deemed "amicable" by the adults. Children see things differently.

Therefore we simply cannot be neutral about marriage. We simply cannot assume that unhappy people mean unsalvageable marriages. And we simply cannot assume that children will be happy if the adults are happy. These are myths.

I believe that anyone working with couples should be able to provide basic information about marriage and marriage education. It means explaining why sticking it out is usually (though not always) the best option. It means offering effective principles and skills that give marriages their best chance of survival. Then people can make genuinely informed choices. Freed from the blindfold of non-directiveness, we ought now to be able to do better.

The relative success of mentoring

If there were a competition for robustness of research findings, the case for marriage would rank a clear first, the case for marriage education would rank second, and the case for mentoring would be third. Put another way, the case for marriage is strong enough to win *"beyond reasonable doubt"*. The case for mentoring is strong enough to win only on the *"balance of probabilities"*. This is owing more to the quantity of available research than to the quality of the case. Nonetheless, there is still good support for mentoring from a number of sources.

The first and most obvious piece of evidence is that the idea makes sense. Whereas the concept and structure of counselling is artificial and relatively new, mentoring has an established natural track record spanning across history. To repeat: mentoring is extended family by another name. It's so self-evident, I hardly need to say it. People learn both consciously and unconsciously from observing and interacting with those who have experience.

Formal mentoring among married couples is an attempt to recreate some of the benefits of extended family. New research studies are beginning to undermine the miserly assumption that only professionals or highly trained people can provide effective support for couples – which would presumably mean that friends and relatives have little to offer.

One study (Stanley *et al.*, 2001) found that ordinary lay educators with a minimum of training could deliver a marriage-education programme as well as or better than professionals. You don't need to be a professional to work with couples. Another study (Ebling & Levenson, 2003) found that people with marriage experience – even newly-weds and the newly divorced – were all better than marriage professionals at predicting the future state of a couple's marriage from a short video clip. Remember I said that computer analysis can do this with up to 80–90% accuracy? Apparently, people with personal experience of marriage do it intuitively better than trained professionals. Experience counts for more than expertise when it comes to knowing about marriage.

Regarding evidence to show that mentoring works, there are no studies I know of that compare the effects of mentoring with non-mentoring. However, there is impressive survey evidence that suggests a very strong association between mentoring and fewer divorces. Association is not the same as cause, so it's important not to draw causal conclusions from surveys. It may be that mentoring is the factor that makes people do better. Or it may be that people who do better also tend to do mentoring. Think of an individual study as a single brick. What we need is enough bricks to make a wall of evidence.

The first and biggest brick comes from a US church-based group called Marriage Savers (see their web site www.marriagesavers.org for more information). Marriage Savers is led by a couple called Mike and Harriet McManus, who are probably the most influential pioneers of marriage mentoring in the US. There are others who also do great work, but Mike has especially influenced me and others in the UK Community Family Trust movement. He claims to find an abnormally low rate of divorce throughout churches that apply an across-the-board approach to marriage support. The Marriage Savers approach has now been rolled out in hundreds of cities and thousands of churches. An independent study lends credence to this claim. Cities whose church leaders sign up to this approach through a Community Marriage Policy have shown a subsequent significant reduction in divorce rates as opposed to comparable cities without such a policy (Birch *et al.*, 2004).

Marriage Savers aims to re-establish the importance of marriage, to introduce effective marriage education as a healthy norm, and to apply the mentoring concept to couples getting married, couples in troubled marriages and couples forming stepfamilies. Note the importance of values, learning and support. One of the common themes is the importance of marriage preparation using mentor couples and an inventory. Across six such Marriage Savers churches, comprising 8,000 adults and 560 weddings, there were just thirteen divorces over a three-to-ten-year period. My own analysis suggests that this is between 84% and 92% fewer divorces than there should have been. This is hard to dismiss out of hand. Something unusual is going on.

Two similar bricks can also be added to the wall. An international organisation called Retrouvaille invites couples whose marriages are on the brink to come to a weekend seminar led by couples who have been to the brink and come back. Retrouvaille claims to have restored the marriages of 80% of the 60,000 couples who visited these weekends. There are a lot of questions about this claim. But the sheer numbers add another brick to the wall of evidence in favour of mentoring.

Another organisation, called Marriage Ministries, based in Florida, claims to have restored the marriages of over 90% of 150 couples. The approach used is similar to that of

Alcoholics Anonymous and also relies on couples who have come back from the brink telling their story. A few years ago, my wife, Kate, and I spent a couple of days in the US being trained by Dick and Phyllis McGinnis, who started this inspirational programme. Although we've not used this approach in the UK, it has the smell of plausibility and wisdom attached to it. Some of the stories of couples brought back from the brink are truly astonishing and offer a source of real hope.

There is, of course, scope for scepticism. People doubted Mike McManus' claims that his city marriage policies reduced divorces. Yet this has now been validated. I see no reason to doubt his numbers for church divorces. Whether these church couples are doing better because of other factors has not been tested. However, there is a decent *prima facie* case for believing that couples *"who have been there"* are the people best suited to help couples *"who are there now"* – whether couples getting married, couples who are already married, couples who are on the brink, or couples in stepfamilies. The combined survey evidence from Marriage Savers, Retrouvaille and Marriage Ministries covers an awful lot of couples. Something's going right. Mentoring may be that something.

Given the abundance of survey evidence and a plausible hypothesis, it is odd that there have yet to be any serious studies published on mentoring. Marriage Savers have been around for long enough to encourage somebody to test them – whether to support or discredit. Mentoring studies are certainly long overdue and I trust it's just a matter of time before a decent study appears in one of the marriage journals.

A final piece of indirect evidence in support of mentoring relates to the use of relationship inventories or questionnaires. At least two published studies have found that 10% or more of couples getting married choose to cancel their weddings after completing their inventory programmes (Fowers & Olson, 1986; Williams & Jurich, 1995). Interestingly, the responses of these couples look similar to those who end up unhappy or divorced within a few years of their wedding.

In the UK, 14% of newly-wed couples get divorced within the first five years of marriage. Had they used inventories, it's possible that almost all these couples might have avoided a costly error. So here is a plausible case for suggesting that the reduction in early-marriage divorces found by Marriage Savers is both genuine and due to the weeding effect of inventories.

Those who want to find flaws in the mentoring story can quite rightly point to the lack of hard evidence. The case for mentoring rests on a plausible story, some decent-sized survey data, and some indirect evidence from inventories. I'd be pushed to claim that this is proof beyond reasonable doubt. But it should be enough to win on the balance of probabilities.

Suggested reasons why mentoring works

The Marriage Savers programme appears to have three main ingredients: a public valuing of marriage; the availability of regular ongoing marriage education as a healthy norm, and the availability of regular ongoing support in the form of mentoring. Value, learning and support.

Mentoring itself shares these three ingredients. The act of volunteering to be a mentor shows a couple that their marriage is valued and important. The content of mentoring offers both explicit and implicit social learning opportunities that continue along with the friendship of the mentors and their couple. The process of mentoring offers ongoing support. These ingredients – value, learning and support – represent a rediscovery of the benefits of extended family.

Extended family offers intimate exposure to several couples as a source of reinforced values, role models and support. In contrast, modern nuclear families offer children intimate exposure to just one couple – their parents. Where there is dysfunction between the parents – as is inevitable in all relationships at some level – the children lack an alternative trusted source of values, or role models from whom to learn intimacy, or a source of support in their own relationships.

There is plenty of evidence that relationship behaviours jump to the next generation. For example, Professor Paul Amato's 20-year family study shows very clearly that divorce breeds divorce and marital problems breed marital problems (Amato & De Boer, 2001).

So the way our parents behave influences the way we behave. Where they blow it, we have only their mistakes from which to learn. Mentoring, like extended family, mediates the effects by showing us an alternative marriage at close quarters.

The key messages of both mentoring and extended family are the same:

- Value *"Your marriage is important and worth the time we spend with you"*
- Learning *"It's OK to learn and keep learning about marriage from other couples"*
- Support *"It's OK to talk about our marriage with other couples"*.

Conclusion

Much of our behaviour is determined by how we are brought up. Families give us a sense of values, learning and support. Extended families reinforce these influences. Yet as our labour markets become ever more flexible, so families have become ever more spread out. The values, learning and support that used to be provided almost automatically by uncles and aunts, grandparents and cousins, become less and less common. The state is taking over vital roles and influences as extended families disappear.

Mentoring is an equally influential source of values, learning and support. Apprenticeship has been the way people learn professional trades. Mentoring is popular in schools. There is no reason not to apply the same concept to marriage. Those with more experience act as mentors to those with less experience. This is pretty much what extended families used to do.

Yet the message from the couple-counselling profession puts many people off. If you work with couples, you need to be a trained expert – say the experts. Experts say you mustn't impose your own or any other values. Experts say you mustn't teach couples in a directive manner. Experts say you mustn't reveal much of your own personal experience. Yet these mistaken ideas have infected the way we all think about supporting marriages.

Studies now confirm that you don't need to be an expert to sit down and talk about marriage. In fact, those with experience appear to do a better job than professionals. There is also a great deal of evidence that mentoring works. Surveys find that, where mentoring is used with engaged couples and those in troubled marriages, divorce rates are abnormally low. More evidence is needed to prove this conclusively. But a good story and some good preliminary data present a sufficiently convincing case for the benefits of mentoring.

What is it that makes mentoring so compelling? The very act of mentoring conveys a sense that your marriage is valued. The content of mentoring convinces that marriage can be learned from others' experience, usually of everyday ups and downs. The process of mentoring shows that it's OK to talk to another couple who have been there before you.

We may have lost the extended family. But we can rebuild its major benefits through mentoring. Support couples, like extended family, provide values, learning and support. It's so obviously a good idea.

References

- Amato, P. and De Boer, D. (2001) The transmission of marital instability across generations: Relationship skills or commitment to marriage? *Journal of Marriage and Family* 63, 1038–1051.
- Birch, P., Weed, S. and Olsen, J. (2004) Assessing the impact of community marriage policies on US county divorce rates. *Family Relations* 53, 495–503.
- Booth, A. and Amato, P. (2001) Parental predivorce relations and offspring postdivorce well-being. *Journal of Marriage and Family* 63, 197–212.
- Doherty, W. (1999) How therapy can be hazardous to your marital health. Paper presented at Smartmarriages conference. (See www.smartmarriages.com)
- Ebling, R. and Levenson, R.W. (2003) Who are the marital experts? *Journal of Marriage and Family* 65, 130–142.
- Fowers, B.J. and Olson, D.H. (1986) Predicting marital success with PREPARE: A predictive validity study. *Journal of Marital and Family Therapy* 12, 403–413.
- Gottman, J.M. (1998) Psychology and the study of marital processes. *Annual Review of Psychology* 49, 169–197.
- Prior, P.M. and Hayes, B.C. (2003) The relationship between marital status and health. *Journal of Family Issues* 24, 124–148.
- Stanley, S.M. *et al.*, (2001). Community based pre-marital prevention: Clergy and lay leaders on the front lines. *Family Relations* 50, 67–76.

- Waite, L. *et al.* (2002) *Does Divorce Make People Happy? Findings from a Study of Unhappy Marriages.* New York: Institute for American Values.
- Williams, L. and Jurich, J. (1995) Predicting marital success after five years: Assessing the predictive validity of FOCCUS. *Journal of Marital and Family Therapy* 21, 141–153.

Appendix A Christian principles in marriage research

In this chapter

- Principles behind the case for marriage
- Principles behind the case for marriage education
- Principles behind the case for mentoring

Introduction

Being a support couple is all about marriage and not about faith. Community Family Trusts and other inventory users market through the media and other avenues as well as through churches. Yet, in the UK at least, it is predominantly Christians who are volunteering to become support couples. Although the majority of our engaged couples in Bristol come from non-church sources, only one of our 65 volunteer support couples has come from outside the church.

Therefore, this appendix offers Christian support couples my personal angle on how I reconcile scripture with what the research is telling us. Some of it is original. Some of it is not.

I often meet Christians who are surprised to find the principles in the Bible borne out in everyday life. Yet if God took the trouble to give us principles, they should surely still apply regardless of what our prevailing culture may choose to think.

In Chapter 10 of this book, I showed how research finds that marriage is a good idea and that the alternatives are generally not. The Bible also tells us this.

In Chapter 11, I showed how research finds that successful relationships depend on both negative and positive factors. Research tells us how important attitude is, in particular negative attitude, to relationships. The Bible also tells us this.

In Chapter 12, I showed how research finds that successful relationships benefit from training and support from those with more experience. The Bible also tells us this.

So here are some things I think the Bible has to say that make the case for marriage, the case for marriage education, and the case for mentoring. I hope it will encourage you, as it does me, to see both Bible and research run hand in hand. It may even challenge you to think differently.

Principles behind the case for marriage

All of us have some image in our mind of what a wedding involves. The key image I hold is of my own wedding in 1986. I married Kate in a small country church on a very grand estate on a hot day under a blue sky. The wedding day and the weeks before and after revolved around an endless array of traditions which, thankfully for me, were mostly organised by my bride's mother.

Other people will have very different images of weddings. Some view the traditions that we upheld as outdated and will discard them from their own weddings. Others include new traditions which I would willingly discard – for example, the new trend for handing out party bags of sugared almonds or gifts. To me this adds to an already overinflated mountain of unnecessary costs. In other countries, other wedding traditions abound. Outside Europe, marriage is often an automatic rite of passage conducted with simple ceremony and traditions.

For the last few hundred years, formal weddings in the UK have tended to be slanted towards the church and those more prosperous. But there have also been less formal public ceremonies that reflect a similar commitment to marriage. In the 19th century, a socially accepted alternative to marriage involved hopping over a broom together. The current myth of common-law marriage probably stems from this community acceptance of a couple living together as if married. The cycle may have come full circle now that formal weddings can take place informally while the couple and celebrant are dangling on a parachute after leaping out of an aeroplane!

My point is that societies change and weddings change to reflect the cultural preferences of that society. But marriage, whether a formal public ceremony or an informal community ceremony, remains a constant in all societies. Throughout history, no civilised culture has prevailed that has turned its back on marriage.

Marriage

What is at the core of marriage from a Christian perspective? I think the Bible starts by telling us three things:

- Marriage is the formation of a new family unit
- Marriage is an unbreakable promise
- Marriage is a framework for absolute intimacy and sex.

For this reason a man will leave his father and mother and be united to his wife, and they will become one flesh. The man and his wife were both naked, and they felt no shame. (Genesis 2:24–25)

In my view, this should be the biblical benchmark against which we measure both marriage and its alternatives.

The prophet Malachi elaborates that marriage is based on covenant – an unbreakable promise – and that marriage is for the benefit of children.

> *...she is your partner, the wife of your marriage covenant. Has not the Lord made them one? In flesh and spirit they are his. And why one? Because he was seeking godly offspring.* (Malachi 2:14–15)

This key role of both physical and spiritual bonds helps me to understand why divorce is viewed so negatively in the Bible. Malachi goes on to say this: *" 'I hate divorce,' says the Lord God of Israel, 'and I hate a man's covering himself with violence as well as with his garment,' says the Lord Almighty. So guard yourself in your spirit, and do not break faith"* (Malachi 2:16).

Jesus hardly pulls his punches when quizzed by the Pharisees about whether divorce is OK *"for any and every reason"*.

> *"Haven't you read,"* he replied, *"that at the beginning the Creator 'made them male and female', and said, 'For this reason a man will leave his father and mother and be united to his wife, and the two will become one flesh'? So they are no longer two, but one. Therefore what God has joined together, let man not separate."* (Matthew 19:3–6)

It might therefore be reasonable to conclude that, regardless of our faith, getting and staying married should be good for us and for our families. It's God's original plan. It should work well for all of us. Sure enough, that's what the research finds. Overwhelmingly, married people and their children tend to do better than any other group on every available social indicator.

Divorce

Divorce is a tough issue for Christians. The Bible does not mince its words. We've already seen how in Malachi 2:16 God says *"I hate divorce"*. Some may take comfort from the fact that God continues by saying *"and I hate a man's covering himself with violence"*. Maybe this provides a legitimate exit in cases of abuse – a view offered some support by research. Children generally do better following divorce only where there was a high level of conflict in the marriage.

Jesus makes it clear that a key issue in divorce is adultery:

> *Moses permitted you to divorce your wives because your hearts were hard. But it was not this way from the beginning. I tell you that anyone who divorces his wife, except for marital unfaithfulness, and marries another woman commits adultery.* (Matthew 19:8–9)

Adultery is a central issue in divorce – whether before the divorce or during a subsequent relationship. Proverbs warns how wisdom *"...will save you also from the adulteress, from the wayward wife with her seductive words, who has left the partner of her youth and ignored the covenant she made before God. For her house leads down to death and her paths to the spirits of the dead. None who go to her return or attain the paths of life"* (Proverbs 2:16–19). The writer of Revelation 14:8 equates evil with adultery and prostitution: *"Fallen is Babylon the Great, which made all the nations drink the maddening wine of her adulteries."* Isaiah 1:21 also describes how *"the faithful city has become a harlot"*. It goes on and on.

Theologians disagree on whether adultery is the only reason for divorce. Some argue that Jesus is responding to a specific contemporary debate about whether divorce was permissible for "any" cause. Old Testament law can be viewed as permitting divorce for the withholding of protection or conjugal rights. This would justify divorce on the grounds of neglect or abuse. All agree, however, that divorce is bad news.

I find it helpful to understand why adultery is such a big issue by looking back at God's original plan for marriage. When Genesis 2:24 talks of a man and wife *"united"* together, the writer uses the language of glue. Divorce must therefore involve the tearing of that glued bond, with unavoidable residual damage. Breaking that covenant promise amounts to a breaking of both the physical and the spiritual bonds of marriage. Building a new sexual relationship with somebody else, even in a new marriage, is not what we were designed for.

It might therefore be reasonable to conclude that, regardless of our faith, divorce will not be good for us and for our families. Sure enough, that's what research finds. Overwhelmingly, divorced people and their children tend to do worse than married people on every available social indicator.

Cohabitation

As far as I know, the Bible has little to say directly about cohabitation. The Bible talks at length about the dangers of sexual sin, adultery and prostitution. Leviticus 20:10–21 says that a man shouldn't sleep with *"...another man's wife"*, *"...his father's wife"*, *"...his daughter-in-law"*, *"...a man"*, *"...a woman and her mother"*, *"...an animal"*, *"...his sister"*, *"...his aunt"*, *"...his sister-in-law"*, etc. In other words, sex outside marriage in *any* form is a bad idea. However, the question reverts once again to what constitutes marriage.

I repeat that I think Genesis 2:24–25 suggests three defining features of marriage: formation of a new family unit; an unbreakable promise; and a framework for absolute intimacy and sex. I can narrow this definition further to a combination of *"one flesh"* plus *"covenant"*. Do cohabiting couples live together as one flesh? Unquestionably. Do cohabiting couples live together in covenant? Maybe in some cases. But probably not in most.

For me, the absence of *"covenant"* is the key feature that distinguishes cohabitation from marriage in biblical teaching. Covenant necessarily involves some form of public affirmation of mutual unconditional commitment. Marriage is based on a public promise to stick things out for life no matter what. Cohabitation is invariably based on a private contract to stick things out under certain conditions. That is not covenant.

However, this raises an interesting issue regarding our modern interpretation of marriage. It could be argued that couples who live together having agreed to marry have taken that step of covenant already. This view is supported by research findings. Multiple cohabitees tend to have higher divorce rates and lower marital quality when they do marry than those who have not cohabited. However, cohabitees who are engaged to be married do equally as well in their subsequent marriage as those who have not cohabited (Teachman, 2003).

This is an argument for not getting too wound up about Christian engaged couples who live together. However, it is *not* a recommendation that they *should* live together once engaged. Couples do break off their engagement. Mentoring may even precipitate this. Therefore, the minority of engaged couples who split up having cohabited carry a damaged history of broken sexual relationship with them.

It might be reasonable to conclude that cohabitation can be the equal of marriage in some cases. That will depend entirely on the mutual attitude of unbreakable commitment probably involving some form of public ceremony. For the majority, however, cohabitation will not be good for us and for our families. Sure enough, that's what research finds. Overwhelmingly, cohabiting people and their children tend to do worse than married people on every available social indicator.

Principles behind the case for marriage education

Having outlined why I think the most important aspect of marriage is covenant, let's now look at some biblical principles that enable a marriage covenant to thrive and flourish. Covenant is essentially an exchange where two people strike an unbreakable promise to share in and take on each other's status, possessions and characteristics. Two become one. One flesh. They start as two individuals with individual characteristics. They finish as one new entity with a new set of characteristics.

In the Old Testament – or Old Covenant – God has transferred his powers, benefits and rights to the Israelites. The law then determines the destructive behaviours that cause them to lose the protection of his covenant. In the New Testament – or Covenant – God sends Jesus to satisfy the demands of the law and transfer all his powers, benefits and rights to those who would like to know him. God's grace now operates, under which we all get the protection of this new covenant.

As a specific example, God made a covenant with Abram (Genesis 15 and 17) to give him a son, and through him a nation of direct descendants who would eventually settle in land promised by God. The covenant promise involved a rather bloody ceremony in which Abram walked between cut halves of slaughtered animals. God confirmed his part by cutting through a *"thick and dreadful darkness"* as a *"blazing torch"*. Abram and his wife Sarai got to have part of God's name – the *"H"* in *"YHWH"* – and changed their names to Abraham and Sarah. Circumcision was the required mark of the covenant, a scar that helped all Israelites remember Abraham's promise from God. We wear wedding rings today and walk out together down the aisle for that reason – as a sign to remind us that we are no longer two but one.

So, apart from wedding rings and aisles, what relevance has this for marriage today? My answer is that marriage is still a covenant. We walk down the aisle to make a public promise that applies until death. Marriage remains an exchange of two old identities for one new identity. Marriage remains a sharing of all worldly goods. Marriage remains an exclusive arrangement.

Much of this boils down to attitude and choice. I can't think and behave like I did before I was married. I have to accept you and your differences. I have to think of both of us. I have to do the best for both of us. Should I start focusing my attention and priorities on myself, my rights, my needs, then I am turning my back on the covenant. My marriage should then suffer. That would seem a biblical approach.

Intimacy and conflict

Let us now look at some of these ideas in more detail. First of these is intimacy. In a covenant marriage, as one flesh, both spouses ought to be able to reveal their greatest differences without fear or reservation. Before the Fall in Genesis 3, Adam and Eve lived in this blissful state of the perfect marriage. Living under God's rules, they had absolute intimacy and no conflict. *"The man and his wife were both naked, and they felt no shame"* (Genesis 2:25).

Yet something strange happened after the Fall. When they broke free of God's rules, Adam and Eve became aware of their nakedness and *"hid from the Lord God among the trees of the garden"* (Genesis 3:8). This is odd partly because they must have been aware that God knew exactly what was going on. When questioned by God, Adam explained his actions thus: *"I was afraid because I was naked; so I hid"* (Genesis 3:10). The really odd part is why they hid because of their nakedness. Surely it was the ears that heard the serpent, the eyes that saw, the nose that smelled, the brain that decided, the mouth that tasted and the body that consumed the fruit, that were all guilty of disobeying God? The one part of both Adam and Eve that played no role whatsoever in the Fall was their nakedness. Yet it was awareness of their nakedness that made them afraid.

The answer, courtesy of Scott Stanley in his excellent book *A Lasting Promise*, is that they were concealing their areas of greatest difference. Whereas Adam and Eve were able to reveal their areas of greatest difference before the Fall and live in perfect intimacy, they were afraid of these inevitable differences after the Fall. The result was conflict. Adam blamed Eve. Eve blamed the serpent (Genesis 3:12–13).

In research terms, the key predictors of marital difficulties turn out to be the negative ways in which we handle areas of greatest difference. Marriages heading for trouble do so because the couples involved handle their inevitable differences poorly. Couples in strong marriages handle their inevitable differences well. This is pretty close to what we might conclude if we had only the Adam and Eve story to go on.

We can therefore be absolutely certain that conflict is

inevitable in a marriage, because all men are different from all women – however "compatible" we may or may not think we are. It's not difference or compatibility that's important. It's how we handle it.

Positive and negative attitude

In a covenant arrangement, my attitude towards the covenant is crucial. In order for the covenant to remain intact, I must consider it to be important. My attitude needs to be positive towards it for it to thrive. No matter how badly my spouse might behave, my responsibility is to take the covenant seriously. When I married Kate, I did not make a conditional contract that said *"I marry you, Kate, as long as you treat me right"*. I made an unconditional promise that said *"I marry you, Kate, for better or worse, to love and to cherish, for richer for poorer, in sickness and in health, to death us do part"*. No conditions. How do I keep my promise? Attitude.

Jesus taught about precisely this point when he was teaching about money. Money was not the important thing in life. Our attitude is. *"For where your treasure is, there your heart will be also"* (Matthew 6:21). For me, this is the number-one scripture that I live by. It has transformed my marriage. When Kate and I were at our lowest point, I really didn't feel love for her. But I was terrified of losing our children if I didn't do something. What I did was to put her interests first. Kate became my treasure. My heart followed and I fell in love with her in a completely new way that I am certain I had never previously experienced in the preceding nine years of married life.

This principle of love as a decision that necessarily leads to actions and feelings is undoubtedly the reason why Paul describes love the way he does in his famous chapter on love.

In every case Paul talks of love as a decision, an action and a choice and NEVER as a feeling – contrary to all popular views of love. Love is *"patient...kind...does not envy...does not boast... is not proud...does not delight in evil...rejoices with the truth... protects...trusts...hopes...perseveres...never fails...And now these three remain: faith, hope and love. But the greatest of these is love"* (1 Corinthians 13:4–13). Love depends on my attitude and not on my feeling. That is rooted in covenant. Positive attitude is positive for relationships.

The flip side of this is negative attitude – in particular, contempt. Two biblical examples illustrate this well. From the Old Testament is a story of the Israelite King David dancing wildly and exuberantly when he returns with the ark of God's covenant. As he does so, his wife Michal sees him leaping about in an undignified manner. *"And when she saw King David leaping and dancing before the Lord, she despised him in her heart"* (2 Samuel 6:16). She then compounds her bad attitude by complaining facetiously to him: *"How the king of Israel has distinguished himself today, disrobing in the sight of the slave girls of his servants as any vulgar fellow would"* (2 Samuel 6:20). Unfortunately, David reacts badly to this contempt and their marriage suffers for it. *"And Michal daughter of Saul had no children to the day of her death"* (2 Samuel 6:23).

From the New Testament comes an example of the dangers of contempt from Jesus' sermon on the mount. Jesus states that the beginning of the path to murder is our attitude. He says this: *"But I tell you that anyone who is angry with his brother will be subject to judgment. Again, anyone who says to his brother, 'Raca', is answerable to the Sanhedrin. But anyone who says, 'You fool!' will be in danger of the fire of hell"* (Matthew 5:22). Swearing in anger is unlawful. But showing contempt, bitterness or invalidation in anger is far more destructive.

Perhaps we should not be surprised to find the Bible

telling us the same thing that the top research groups tell us. Contempt – or bad attitude – is the single most destructive force in a marriage.

Positive and negative behaviour

Following in the footsteps of attitude comes behaviour. Once again, the key is that both negative and positive factors affect marriage and relationships. This idea of negative and positive is one of the strongest of all biblical themes. Once you have recognised it, you will see it in virtually any chapter you care to flick through.

DO NOT do the negative. And DO do the positive.

Let's start at the beginning. Within the Old Testament, the Ten Commandments involve eight DO NOTS and two DOS (Deuteronomy 5:6–21). Do not *"have other gods," "make idols," "misuse God's name," "murder," "commit adultery," "steal," "give false testimony"* and *"covet"*. Do *"observe the Sabbath"* and *"honour your father and mother"*. Two things are especially interesting to me about this. First, the emphasis is on so many more negatives to avoid. Research confirms the greater impact of negatives. Second, the commandments mention adultery rather than divorce. This seems to affirm Jesus' point that adultery is a more significant issue rather than divorce (Matthew 19:8, 9).

Psalms and Proverbs are awash with this contrast between negative and positive. The Psalms even start off with a DO NOT and a DO. *"Blessed is the man who does not walk in the counsel of the wicked... But his delight is in the law of the Lord"* (Psalm 1:1–2). Psalm 1 continues with this theme of contrasting the wise with the foolish. Proverbs is full of the same thing. I picked one Proverb almost at random: *"Better a poor man whose walk is blameless than a fool whose lips are per-*

verse" (Proverbs 19:1). There are hundreds of them. The prophets continue the theme. Isaiah, for example, starts with this warning: *"Stop doing wrong, learn to do right!"* (Isaiah 1:16–17) and then alternates throughout his book between the individual consequences of each.

Moving to the New Testament, Paul in particular elaborates on this point endlessly throughout all his letters. DON'T do the negative and DO do the positive. He talks of how we change from negative to positive when we become Christians. He talks of being *"dead to sin but alive to God in Christ Jesus"* (Romans 6:11). He encourages us to *"put off [the] old self"* and *"put on the new"* (Ephesians 4:22–24). In Colossians 3:1–17, Paul tells us to get rid of the bad and to put on the good: *"Put to death, therefore,....sexual immorality, impurity, lust,"* etc., and *"clothe yourselves with compassion, kindness..."* etc. He spells this out even more obviously in Romans: *"Do not conform any longer to the pattern of this world, but be transformed by the renewing of your mind"* (Romans 12:2). And again: *"Hate what is evil; cling to what is good... Bless and do not curse... Do not be proud, but be willing to associate with people of low position... Do not repay anyone evil for evil. Be careful to do what is right in the eyes of everybody... Do not take revenge, my friends, but leave room for God's wrath... Do not be overcome by evil, but overcome evil with good"* (Romans 12:9–21).

My observation is that many marriage education courses overlook this dual approach and focus mostly or only on building up the positive, wrongly assuming that it will automatically cut out the negative. It doesn't. You may remember from Chapter 11 that I showed how few marriage courses have yet demonstrated an effect on divorce rates. They may well reduce divorce. It may simply be a limitation of the research. But I've often wondered whether there is a more uncomfortable truth at work here.

Courses that focus exclusively on the positive aspects of marriage – whether issues or skills – may be genuinely failing to reduce the negative behaviours linked to divorce. I think PREP is so successful at reducing divorce precisely because it specifically focuses on both negative and positive aspects.

Communication

Because most people would say that good communication is at the centre of healthy relationships, you might think the Bible has much to say about the importance of good communication. In fact, while there is plenty on attitude and behaviour, I can find relatively little on communication. To me this reflects the far greater importance of attitude and behaviour. Good communication is largely a reflection of these things rather than a special skill learned on a course.

However, the Bible does have some things to say. I think you'll agree that even these are couched in the language of attitude.

For me, the active listening skills taught by most marriage courses – and most counselling courses – are intended to build a style that imitates a positive attitude. Paul tells us to *"accept one another, then, just as Christ accepted you, in order to bring praise to God"* (Romans 15:7). He also says: *"Do not let unwholesome talk come out of your mouths, but only what is helpful for building others up according to their needs"* (Ephesians 4:29). This is undoubtedly about good communicating and relationships. But then so is the catch-all command *"Love your neighbour as yourself"*. Are these communication skills? Maybe.

Perhaps the most specific communication skill taught in the Bible comes from James: *"Everyone should be quick to listen, slow to speak and slow to become angry"* (James 1:19). James goes on to warn about speaking carelessly: *"If anyone considers himself religious and yet does not keep a tight rein on his tongue,…his religion is worthless"* (James 1:26). *"Out of the same mouth come praise and cursing. My brothers, this should not be"* (James 3:10).

This suggests to me another hard truth shown up by research. Communication is only one of the factors that predict divorce yet it is often the only factor promoted by marriage educators. The Bible talks so much more about attitude and behaviour – separating negative and positive. There is no disagreement between research and Bible. There's a lesson to be learned here, I think.

Principles behind the case for marriage mentoring

The final case I want to make is probably the easiest one. The benefits of mentoring are largely self-evident once you've heard the basic idea. Mentoring is simply the transfer of experience from those who have more to those who have less. That way, we don't have to repeat others' mistakes as well as our own!

There are some obvious examples of mentoring in the Bible. Jesus disciples his followers throughout the gospels with demonstration and explanation. I hardly need give references for this as you can find plenty of examples for yourself.

I think the most specific example of mentoring comes from Paul in his letter to Titus.

You must teach what is in accordance with sound doctrine. Teach the older men to be temperate, worthy of respect, self-controlled, and sound in faith, in love and in endurance. Likewise, teach the older women to be reverent in the way they live, not to be slanderers or addicted to much wine, but to teach what is good. Then they can train the younger women to love their husbands and children, to be self-controlled and pure, to be busy at home, to be kind, and to be subject to their husbands, so that no one will malign the word of God. Similarly, encourage the young men to be self-controlled. In everything set them an example by doing what is good. In your teaching show integrity, seriousness and soundness of speech that cannot be condemned, so that those who oppose you may be ashamed because they have nothing bad to say about us. (Titus 2:1–8)

Paul could be explaining here pretty much how I run courses in Bristol! I teach the older men and women to be support couples. I encourage the younger men and women who are starting out on their life together. The older men and women then teach or train the younger men and women and set an example for them to follow as they are mentoring. I also try to be serious and show integrity while I'm running the courses! So thank you, Paul, for this model.

In order to help others, I see that Jesus and Paul both stress the importance of training and experience – through demonstration, explanation, encouragement, and practice. What I don't see is any need for special professional skills or expertise to help couples.

I also see both Jesus and Paul using very ordinary people to pass on their experience through teaching and example. What I don't see is evidence of selection based on special intellectual or personal qualities. Anybody with a bit of experience and a bit of training can be a mentor.

Conclusion

I apologise that for many people this appendix will be thoroughly inadequate or inappropriate. For scholars, I won't have said enough. For those damaged by painful marriages, I will have said too much. For non-Christians, I shouldn't have said anything in the first place.

One thing is for certain: I've left out all sorts of important and helpful biblical passages, partly because I've missed them and partly because I don't want to fill the book with too much by way of Christian apologetics. For example, I know that marriage is also a reflection of the relationship between Jesus and the church. There is therefore much to be learned from looking at how Jesus and the church treat each other and applying that to our own marriages. It does much to dispel the distorted view of marriage carried by those who only hear Christians exhorting wives to submit to their horrible husbands. The truth is that Paul also asks husbands to love their wives as Christ loved the church (Ephesians 5:22–33). This is as much a demand on husbands as on wives, and reflects the nature of oneness in the marriage covenant. Kate and I once did an excellent yet intensive course called Married for Life, which focused on exactly this theme.

Interestingly, new research finds that men who sacrifice individual pursuits for their marriage have more committed relationships (Whitton *et al.*, 2002). Whether women sacrifice or not doesn't tell you much, perhaps because women do it naturally. When husbands sacrifice, they most closely fit the Christ/husband and church/wife model of marriage.

Equally, I haven't said much about Paul's instructions on Christian marriage, mostly covering sex, marriage and death (1 Corinthians 7:1–40). Nor have I said much about Peter's very helpful instructions to those with non-Christian spouses (1 Peter 3:1–7).

I hope that what I have included, however, is both encouraging and challenging. The big message is that what God says about marriage in the Bible is reflected accurately in what research finds in real life. Belief is not the important thing here. The principles of marriage have applied to all cultures throughout all of history, regardless of belief. God's principles apply as much today as they did thousands of years ago.

What I see is that the case for marriage is made by God and confirmed by research. Marriage essentially comprises covenant and one flesh. Being designed by God for the wellbeing of our families, it is not surprising to find that marriage is good for us. On the other hand, breaking that covenant causes damage. When one flesh tries to separate back to its component parts, there is inevitable tearing and damage. No wonder divorce is therefore usually bad for us and that subsequent relationships do not do as well. Not committing to some form of covenant in the first place also reduces the effectiveness of our relationship. Cohabitation is certainly one flesh. Whether it is a covenant depends on the individuals. In the majority of cases it is not surprising to find that cohabitation is not good for us.

I see also that the case for marriage education rests on our attitude and resulting behaviour. The Bible demonstrates the importance of both. Positive attitudes are good for marriages because they lead to positive behaviour. Negative attitudes, however, are especially destructive and lead to a spiralling downward cycle. These are exactly what research finds to be the key factors in marital success and failure. For successful marriage, we must focus on both taking off the old and putting on the new. The old self will take over in time unless it is recognised and put down. Learning how to be nice or to communicate well in marriage is never enough. The Bible spends little time talking about communication. Rather, the focus is almost always on attitude and behaviour.

Finally, a clear instruction for mentoring is made by Paul. He encourages older men and older women to be taught various qualities. He then encourages these older men and women to teach or train younger men and women.

Research has made great progress in recent years. It is now finally catching up with what the Bible has been saying for thousands of years. Marriage is good for us. Attitude and behaviour are very important in this. Those with more experience rather than expertise are the ones to pass this on to those with less experience.

References

- Teachman, J. (2003) Premarital sex, premarital cohabitation, and the risk of subsequent marital dissolution among women. *Journal of Marriage and Family* 65, 444–455.
- Whitton, S.W., Stanley, S. M. and Markman, H. J. (2002) Sacrifice in romantic relationships: An exploration of relevant research and theory. In H.T. Reis, M.A. Fitzpatrick, and A.L. Vangelisti (eds) *Stability and Change in Relationship Behavior Across the Lifespan* (pp. 156–181). Cambridge, England: Cambridge University Press.

Appendix B Aide memoire for support couples

Relax !

- Think of yourselves as well-informed "uncle and aunt" figures
- You are not there as "experts"
- Your couple do the work, not you
- It won't matter if you get something wrong.

Stick to your ground rules

- Respect each other – don't dump unexpected issues out of the blue
- Respect privacy and confidentiality – don't discuss your couple with others
- Respect timing – try to start and finish on time.

Be direct

- Get the couple to talk to each other rather than to you
- If an issue takes too much time, suggest they write it down and discuss it during the week
- Interrupt miscommunications and encourage them to paraphrase

- Coach them through the problem-solving method if they get stuck.

Affirm and reinforce

- Encourage them frequently and specifically – *"What you guys are doing really well is…"*
- Use your own examples to suggest ways of doing things differently. *"When we first married, we had much the same problem. The way we dealt with it was…"*

Point out patterns

- Highlight negative attitudes – STOP signs – Scoring Points, Thinking the Worst, Opting Out, Putting Down
- Coach positive attitudes – Love Languages – Time, Words, Actions, Gifts, Touch
- Be aware of eye contact and body language – *"John, I've noticed that whenever Jane talks about…, you seem to…"*
- Use "The Dance" for repeating patterns.

Model good communication yourselves

- Use open questions – *"How… What…"*
- Start sentences with *"I…"* rather than *"You…"*
- Show understanding by paraphrasing – *"So what you're saying is…"*

Don't

- Argue – it's your experience and not your opinion that counts

- Criticise – give your own example if you need to illustrate another way of doing things
- Counsel – get them to talk to each other more than to you
- Gossip – keep your discussions private and confidential.

Know your limits

- If you get stuck, it's a sign of strength to admit you don't know how to handle it
- Ask other relationship educators for advice or ideas, but keep names and details private
- There are excellent books on most subjects
- Consider referring the couple to their GP or a counsellor.

Appendix C   **Details of inventory providers**

FOCCUS (Facilitating Open Couple Communication, Understanding and Study)

FOCCUS
Quel Bec
Cothelstone
TAUNTON
Somerset
TA4 3ED
UNITED KINGDOM
Tel: 01823 432420
www.foccus.co.uk

FOCCUS, Inc.
3214 N. 60th St
Omaha,
Nebraska
68104-3495
UNITED STATES
Tel: 877-833-5422 (Toll Free)
www.foccusinc.com

Approximate costs (2004 prices): The FOCCUS manual on its own costs around UK£25–35 or US$35 plus shipping. Manuals are reusable. Training is optional and costs vary. Processing cost thereafter is around UK£10 or US$15 per couple.

PREPARE/ENRICH

PREPARE/ENRICH UK
SVS
Kingsland Square
Southampton
SO14 1NW
UNITED KINGDOM
Tel: 023 8021 6003
www.prepare-enrich.co.uk

Life Innovations
PO Box 190
Minneapolis,
MN 55440-0190
UNITED STATES
Tel: 800-331-1661 (Toll free)
www.prepare-enrich.com

Approximate costs (2004 prices): Training for PREPARE–ENRICH includes manuals and costs around UK£75 or US$150. Manuals are reusable. Processing cost thereafter is around UK£11–25 or US$35 per couple.